Concussions

Diseases and Disorders

ReferencePoint
Press®

San Diego, CA

Select books in the Compact Research Diseases and Disorders set:

Anorexia
Anxiety Disorders
Asthma
Bipolar Disorders
Depressive Disorders
Impulse Control Disorders
Mood Disorders
Obsessive-Compulsive Disorder
Personality Disorder
Post-Traumatic Stress Disorder
Self-Injury Disorder
Sports Injuries

*For a complete list of titles please visit www.referencepointpress.com.

COMPACT *Research*

Concussions

Peggy J. Parks

Diseases and Disorders

ReferencePoint
Press®

San Diego, CA

© 2014 ReferencePoint Press, Inc.
Printed in the United States

For more information, contact:
ReferencePoint Press, Inc.
PO Box 27779
San Diego, CA 92198
www.ReferencePointPress.com

Picture credits:
Cover: Dreamstime and iStockphoto.com
Maury Aaseng: 33–35, 47–49, 61–62, 75–77
AP Images: 15, 17

LIBRARY OF CONGRESS CATALOGING-IN-PUBLICATION DATA

Parks, Peggy J., 1951–
  Concussions / by Peggy J. Parks.
    pages cm. -- (Compact research series)
  Audience: Grade 9 to 12.
  ISBN 978-1-60152-512-3 (hardback) -- ISBN 1-60152-512-5 (hardback)
    1. Brain--Concussion--Juvenile literature. 2. Sports injuries--Prevention--Juvenile literature.
I. Title.
  RC394.C7P39   2013
  617.1'027--dc23
                                                                          2012043650

Contents

Foreword

"Where is the knowledge we have lost in information?"

—T.S. Eliot, "The Rock."

As modern civilization continues to evolve, its ability to create, store, distribute, and access information expands exponentially. The explosion of information from all media continues to increase at a phenomenal rate. By 2020 some experts predict the worldwide information base will double every seventy-three days. While access to diverse sources of information and perspectives is paramount to any democratic society, information alone cannot help people gain knowledge and understanding. Information must be organized and presented clearly and succinctly in order to be understood. The challenge in the digital age becomes not the creation of information, but how best to sort, organize, enhance, and present information.

ReferencePoint Press developed the *Compact Research* series with this challenge of the information age in mind. More than any other subject area today, researching current issues can yield vast, diverse, and unqualified information that can be intimidating and overwhelming for even the most advanced and motivated researcher. The *Compact Research* series offers a compact, relevant, intelligent, and conveniently organized collection of information covering a variety of current topics ranging from illegal immigration and deforestation to diseases such as anorexia and meningitis.

The series focuses on three types of information: objective single-author narratives, opinion-based primary source quotations, and facts and statistics. The clearly written objective narratives provide context and reliable background information. Primary source quotes are carefully selected and cited, exposing the reader to differing points of view, and facts and statistics sections aid the reader in evaluating perspectives. Presenting these key types of information creates a richer, more balanced learning experience.

For better understanding and convenience, the series enhances information by organizing it into narrower topics and adding design features that make it easy for a reader to identify desired content. For example, in *Compact Research: Illegal Immigration*, a chapter covering the economic impact of illegal immigration has an objective narrative explaining the various ways the economy is impacted, a balanced section of numerous primary source quotes on the topic, followed by facts and full-color illustrations to encourage evaluation of contrasting perspectives.

The ancient Roman philosopher Lucius Annaeus Seneca wrote, "It is quality rather than quantity that matters." More than just a collection of content, the *Compact Research* series is simply committed to creating, finding, organizing, and presenting the most relevant and appropriate amount of information on a current topic in a user-friendly style that invites, intrigues, and fosters understanding.

Concussions at a Glance

Concussions Defined

A concussion is a mild traumatic brain injury that affects the brain's normal functioning.

How Concussions Occur

A concussion can result when someone sustains a blow to the head or body, causing the brain to bounce around inside the head and bang into the hard, bony skull.

Warning Signs

The most obvious signs of concussion are dizziness, nausea, blurred vision, and problems with balance, although symptoms may vary depending on the severity of the injury.

Nonsports Causes

The most common causes of concussion are motor vehicle accidents and falls.

Concussion-Prone Sports

The risk of concussion is greatest in sports that involve intentional blows to the head (mixed martial arts and boxing) and contact sports such as football and hockey.

Prevalence

The Centers for Disease Control and Prevention (CDC) estimates that between 1.7 million and 3.8 million people in the United States sustain some form of traumatic brain injury each year, most of which are concussions.

Diagnosis and Treatment

Concussions are diagnosed based on symptoms, and the only treatment is complete physical and cognitive rest until the brain has healed.

Risks

Concussions may lead to long-term problems such as memory loss and depression; cumulative damage from concussions can result in severe brain deterioration and a condition known as chronic traumatic encephalopathy.

Prevention

Athletic organizations and schools throughout the United States have adopted policies to help prevent concussions, and legislation to help protect youth athletes has been passed in forty-one states and Washington, DC.

Overview

> **The signs and symptoms of a concussion can be subtle and may not be immediately apparent. Symptoms can last for days, weeks or even longer.**
>
> —Mayo Clinic, a world-renowned medical facility headquartered in Rochester, Minnesota.

> **It's important to understand exactly what a concussion is. It is a complex, functional disturbance of the brain that results from a traumatic force.**
>
> —Mandy Huggins, a sports medicine physician from South Florida.

Zach Brady is a teenager from Vancouver, Washington, who has loved the game of football since he was a little boy. By the time he got to high school, Brady was a standout defensive linebacker who dreamed of playing college ball after graduation. Throughout his years of playing football, he had sustained a number of concussions. But like most young athletes, he put the team first, ignored the pain, and went back to the game—until the summer of 2011, when a concussion at football camp took a devastating toll on his brain and shattered his dreams for a football career.

After the concussion Brady not only lost the ability to play the sport he loved, he also missed out on most of his senior year. Being at school was impossible because he could not focus and easily became overwhelmed by the activity and noise in the hallways. For months he had to stay home and take online classes. Above all, Brady became terribly frustrated that his brain no longer worked the way it had before. Whereas in the past he was a top student who spent no more than an hour writing essays that easily earned A grades, the papers he wrote after his last concussion took ten times as long to complete. Worse yet, he found it devastating to go back and read them afterward and see how jumbled his reasoning was. "I wish I just had a bunch of broken bones," says Brady, "and it could heal."[1]

Protected Yet Vulnerable

To understand how concussions affect the brain, it helps to have an understanding of how the brain works. For an organ that weighs only about 3 pounds (1.4 kg), the brain holds an extraordinary amount of power. It is composed of billions of interconnecting cells (known as neurons) that constantly communicate with each other through rapid-fire electrical signals. These signals, which are facilitated by chemicals known as neurotransmitters, allow the brain to regulate everything from intelligence, emotions, sense of humor, and memory to movement and behavior. Neurosurgeon Keith Black writes: "Unlike any other organ in the body, our brain is the essence of what makes us human, our memories, our thoughts, our personalities—one hundred billion nerve cells, working in absolute harmony to allow us to see, to smell, to move, to understand, and to create."[2]

The brain is soft, gelatin-like, and fragile, but is protected in several ways. The first line of protection is the meninges (or meningeal layers), which include three layers of membrane: the pia mater (innermost layer next to the brain), the arachnoid layer (middle), and the dura mater (outermost layer). Wrapped in the meninges and encased inside the hard, bony skull (or cranium), the brain floats in a layer of cerebrospinal fluid, which cushions it like a liquid shock absorber. Together, these protective mechanisms do a good job of shielding the brain from normal everyday bumps and jolts—but it is still vulnerable to serious injury.

What Are Concussions?

The word *concussion* is derived from the Latin verb *concutere*, which means "to shake violently." This is a fitting description of what happens during a concussion: an outside force causes the brain to bounce around inside the skull and bump into its hard, bony surface. This is most common when an individual sustains a blow to the head, but concussion can also result from a hit to the body or a whiplash-type injury that throws the head forward and backward. To illustrate this phenomenon, sports medicine physician Andrew M. Blecher uses the metaphor of an egg: "If you take an egg and shake it around, what happens to the yolk inside? You may not damage the shell by shaking the egg but the yolk moves around freely due to the acceleration and deceleration forces from the shaking. This motion of the yolk within the shell damages the yoke as it bangs up against the shell. . . . The same thing occurs in the brain."[3]

> **The word *concussion* is derived from the Latin verb *concutere*, which means 'to shake violently.'**

Concussions are included in the category of traumatic brain injuries and are the most common type. In medical literature concussions are defined as mild traumatic brain injuries. Although this is often interpreted to mean they are not serious, that is an incorrect assumption. Rather, *mild* refers to how concussions compare to more severe brain injuries. In her book *Ahead of the Game*, neuropsychologist and concussion expert Rosemarie Scolaro Moser writes:

> Concussions are considered mild brain injuries because there is no skull fracture, there is no intracranial bleeding or hemorrhaging, and recovery is expected. But that doesn't mean that concussion is not *serious*. After all, you'd take even a 'mild' heart attack seriously, wouldn't you? The same principle applies to concussions.[4]

Concussion Warning Signs

Brain trauma experts say that people who sustain concussions are often unaware of the injury because they are not familiar with the symptoms. A widespread belief is that in order for someone to have a concussion, he or she must be knocked unconscious. This is not true, however, as Julian Bailes, a neurosurgeon who directs the Brain Injury Research Institute, explains: "With the vast majority of concussions in sports—90 percent of the time, in fact—athletes don't get knocked out. They're walking around and talking, and they look normal."[5] According to Bailes, the mistaken belief that a concussion has occurred only if a player becomes unconscious is not only incorrect, it is dangerous.

Concussion symptoms are divided into four categories: physical, cognition/memory, emotional/mood, and sleep disturbances. Common physical symptoms include headache, fuzzy or blurry vision, sensitivity to noise and/or light, dizziness, feeling tired and lacking energy, and problems with balance. Warning signs related to cognition/memory include difficulty thinking clearly, feeling slowed down, trouble concentrating, and difficulty remembering new information. Emotional/mood symptoms include irritability, inexplicable sadness, nervousness and/or anxiety, and sleep disturbances are interruptions in normal sleep patterns.

Nonsports Causes

Although concussions are typically associated with sports and recreational activities, these injuries can and do happen in a variety of different ways. Reports by the CDC show that motor vehicle accidents are the most common cause of concussions, which health officials say often result from people not wearing seat belts. A 2012 study by the Trust for America's Health and the Robert Wood Johnson Foundation found that eighteen US states do not have seat belt laws in place. These states have injury rates (including concussions) that are significantly higher than states with seat belt legislation in place. Mehmet Oz, who is vice chair and professor of surgery at Columbia University, writes: "Always wear your seat belt, since automobile accidents are one of the more common causes of concussions—as any physician who has worked a shift in the ER could tell you."[6]

> " **Brain trauma experts say that people who sustain concussions are often unaware of the injury because they are not familiar with the symptoms.** "

Another leading cause of concussions is accidental falls, which are responsible for the majority of concussions in elderly people and children. The two-year-old daughter of Jeffrey Kluger, who is senior editor for *Time* magazine, sustained a concussion after colliding with another child on the patio of a museum in Mexico City. After the collision Elisa Kluger fell down on her bottom, tipped backward, and then hit her head on the patio. Kluger writes: "The sound was one that parents dread: the singular clunk of skull striking cement. I winced, Elisa wailed, and I gathered her up."[7] About twenty minutes later the little girl became uncharacteristically withdrawn, started to vomit, and went into convulsions. Kluger and his wife rushed her to the hospital, where she was diagnosed with a concussion.

Concussion-Prone Sports

The risk for concussions is greatest in sports that involve intentional blows to the head, such as in mixed martial arts and boxing. Ken Reed, a physician and sports policy director for the sports reform organization League of Fans, writes: "Boxing, of course, is the ultimate sport for concussions. The goal is to knock out your opponent, in effect, to give the other person a concussion." Reed goes on to say that the popularity of boxing has lagged over the years, so sports such as hockey and football have "moved to the forefront when the subject of concussions in sports is brought up."[8] The number one sport for concussions is football, with hockey, lacrosse, rugby, and basketball also having a high incidence of concussions among players.

> **The risk for concussions is greatest in sports that involve intentional blows to the head, such as in mixed martial arts and boxing.**

Even sports that are not hard-hitting collision sports have a high prevalence of concussions. Soccer, for instance, is the number one source of concussions among female athletes. One major reason for the high concussion rate is the practice of heading, in which players use their heads to direct the ball. Says Robert C. Cantu, who is a Boston neurosurgeon and world-renowned expert on sports-related concussions: "People who think of concussions as only being present mostly in guys and mostly in the sport of football are just plain wrong. Soccer is right at the top of the list for girls."[9] Because of the dangers associated with heading, Cantu recommends that the practice be eliminated from all youth soccer.

Among high school students, boys' sports account for 75 percent of all concussions, and football accounts for more than half of all concussions in high school sports. The usual cause of sports-related concussions is a blow to the head.

Concussion Prevalence

Health officials can make estimates about the number of concussions that occur each year, but they have no way of knowing the exact figure. That is largely because such data are compiled based on visits to emergency rooms, and most concussion sufferers never seek medical care. Says Julie Gilchrist, a physician with the CDC's National Center for Injury Prevention and Control: "There's a vast undercounting of the concussions in the general population."[10] According to the CDC, an estimated 1.7 million to 3.8 million people in the United States sustain some form of traumatic brain injury each year, with about 75 percent of those injuries being concussions. In a December 2011 paper, the American Association of Neurological Surgeons stated that more than three hundred thousand concussions occur each year as a result of sports-related injuries.

Research consistently shows that concussions are a serious problem among youth who participate in sports. In high school sports alone, for example, the CDC estimates that more than sixty-two thousand concussions occur each year. But since concussions are underreported, even in youth sports, health officials believe that the actual number is significantly higher. In his book, *Kids, Sports, and Concussions*, Boston physician and brain trauma expert William Paul Meehan III writes: "Since a concussion cannot be 'seen,' athletes are able to conceal it from athletic trainers, team physicians, coaches, and parents. And many of them do." Meehan refers to a study of football players from American high schools that showed less than half who sustained a concussion reported it to anyone. "Many younger athletes do not realize they have sustained a concussion," he says. "Fewer realize that a concussion is a traumatic brain injury. They believe they have merely 'had their bell rung' or been 'dinged.'"[11]

The Female Factor

In sports played by both males and females, studies have shown that gender plays a role in who is most vulnerable to concussions. In at least two sports, basketball and soccer, female athletes sustain significantly more concussions than males. One report, which was published in a 2008 issue of the *Journal of Athletic Training*, showed that girls playing high school soccer suffered concussions 68 percent more often than boys who played soccer, and rates for basketball were nearly three times higher for female players. Although researchers are not clear on the reasons for this discrepancy, one theory is that females have weaker neck muscles than males. Cantu explains: "Girls as a group have far weaker necks. The same force delivered to a girl's head spins the head much more because of the weak neck than it does the guy's."[12]

> " Along with having a higher risk of sustaining concussions, females typically take longer to recover from the injuries. "

Along with having a higher risk of sustaining concussions, females typically take longer to recover from the injuries. This was one of the findings of a study that appeared in the June 1, 2012, issue of the *American Journal of Sports Medicine*. The research team, led by Tracey Covassin of Michigan State University, followed a group of high school and college athletes

Soccer is the number one source of concussions among female athletes. The high concussion rate is linked to the practice of heading the ball. Some medical experts have called for the elimination of this practice from all youth soccer.

for two years. They found that the female athletes who suffered concussions exhibited more symptoms and showed greater declines in cognitive skills than the male athletes in the study. Says Covassin: "Parents need to understand that if their daughter has a concussion, that they may potentially take longer to recover from that concussion than their son who is a football player."[13]

How Are Concussions Diagnosed and Treated?

Many types of injuries can be confirmed or ruled out by diagnostic testing; however, no such tests currently exist for concussions. This is true even of scanning technology such as computed tomography (CT) and magnetic resonance imaging (MRI), as Meehan explains: "Although the signs and symptoms of a concussion can be serious . . . it can be hard to see them when you look at images of concussed brains; CT scans and MRIs often don't clearly show how a concussed brain has been injured. There's no bruising, no bleeding and no swelling."[14] When a concussion is suspected, the physician takes a medical history, which includes asking detailed questions about how the injury occurred, and performs a complete physical examination. A concussion diagnosis is made based on symptoms and the patient's responses to visual and verbal stimuli, such as tests that gauge balance, thinking skills, and memory.

Just as no tests can precisely diagnose a concussion, there are no drugs or medical procedures specifically designed to help someone overcome the injury. Rather, the only "treatment" is complete rest. This includes avoiding not only physical exertion and exercise but also activities that require mental concentration. Cantu explains: "People have not been so aware of the need for resting the brain. Individuals with cognitive concussion symptoms who exert their brain by doing computer work, reading, doing lengthy homework assignments, playing video games, texting will exacerbate their symptoms in almost every instance."[15] Such restrictive requirements can be extremely difficult for patients, especially children and teens who are used to being active, but complete rest is essential for the brain to recover.

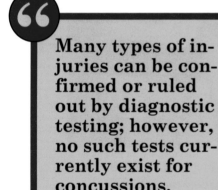

> Many types of injuries can be confirmed or ruled out by diagnostic testing; however, no such tests currently exist for concussions.

Lingering Effects

As serious as concussions can be, most sufferers recover fully in a relatively short time. Brain trauma specialists say that up to 85 percent of concussion sufferers are able to recover within two weeks if they rest and are careful not to be injured again. For some, however, symptoms linger for a much longer period, as sports medicine physician Mandy Huggins explains: "For reasons still not completely clear, some will go on to experience post-concussion syndrome (PCS), which is diagnosed when symptoms persist, sometimes for months or even years."[16]

> **The most dangerous risk of sustaining a second concussion before the brain has properly healed from the first is the development of second-impact syndrome.**

This was the case with Lacey, a young woman living in Canada. In September 2011 she sustained a concussion after losing her balance and hitting her head on the bathroom sink. Nearly a year after the injury, she continued to feel emotionally unstable, suffered from headaches, and had anxiety attacks whenever she was in chaotic environments or heard loud noises. Lacey wrote in June 2012:

> I'm struggling, and that frustrates me. I've been to a few doctors about these issues and each time they say there is nothing they can do for me because the problems are caused by my post concussion syndrome, not a chemical imbalance or an inability to cope with a crisis. They say this could last from a few months, to several years, or the rest of my life. I wish I could take a pill for a while, or get some counseling and be better. But those remedies won't help me.[17]

What Are the Risks of Concussions?

Although any brain injury involves a certain amount of risk, concussions usually do not lead to serious problems or long-term complications. The American Association of Neurological Surgeons writes: "In most cases, a single concussion should not cause permanent damage."[18] After suffering a concussion, patients are at greatest risk when they fail to abstain from mental and physical activity for a long enough period. This is especially true if they return to sports and put themselves in danger of further blows to the head or body.

The most dangerous risk of sustaining a second concussion before the brain has properly healed from the first is the development of second-impact syndrome. This is a rare but devastating condition, as Meehan explains:

> Every year during football season, there is an article in the newspaper about an athlete who returned to football before he had recovered completely from a concussion. Often, the athlete told his doctor, athletic trainer, and coach that he was better but confided to friends and teammates that he still had some lingering symptoms, such as headaches or nausea. And, although no one remembers any major blows to the head or collisions, the athlete develops massive brain swelling and dies.[19]

Meehan goes on to say that the athletes who have survived second-impact syndrome have been left severely brain damaged and disabled by the condition.

Can Sports-Related Concussions Be Prevented?

Helmets and other protective gear have become much more sophisticated over the years and can help prevent many types of serious injuries, including skull fractures. But whether the same is true of protecting against concussions is a topic of controversy. Many experts argue that even top-rated helmets lined with state-of-the-art padding cannot stop the brain from banging into the skull if someone sustains a blow to the body or head. Mark Lovell, a neuropsychologist from Pittsburgh, Pennsylvania, who cocreated a well-known diagnostic test called ImPACT, explains: "The brain is still moving around within the skull when somebody has a concussion, and that's what causes them. We can't put a helmet directly on the brain."[20]

Experts say that one of the most important ways to help prevent concussions is through greater public awareness. Reed shares his thoughts: "Coaches and parents are woefully uneducated when it comes to brain injuries. The result is too few concussions are properly identified, and the ones that are don't receive the recommended treatment. Education is critical when it comes to concussions because multiple concussions increase both the short- and long-term risks for young athletes."[21]

In recent years, professional sports organizations have put measures in place to help reduce the incidence of concussions. This is true of the National Football League (NFL) and the National Hockey League (NHL), both of which have initiated rule changes to protect players.

A Troubling Issue

Most concussions are not life-threatening, nor do most lead to long-term complications—but these traumatic brain injuries have the potential to be serious. They can be caused by motor vehicle accidents, falls, and participation in a number of different sports, from football to lacrosse or soccer. Concussions can usually be diagnosed based on symptoms and are treated with rest until the brain is completely healed. Brain trauma experts say that the concussion problem is growing and that the answer is prevention—although how best to reduce the concussion rate remains an issue of debate.

What Are Concussions?

❝It's remarkable how poorly understood concussion remains today considering that the condition was formally identified over a millennium ago.❞

—Linda Carroll and David Rosner, authors of *The Concussion Crisis: Anatomy of a Silent Epidemic*.

❝It's not just full-blown concussions that are a cause for concern. Perhaps the most important recent finding in the area of concussion research is that repetitive small hits to the head can cause as much damage as big blows.❞

—Ken Reed, a physician and sports policy director for the sports reform organization League of Fans.

William Paul Meehan III is a physician who specializes in brain trauma and directs the Sports Concussion Clinic in the Division of Sports Medicine at Boston Children's Hospital. Now in his early forties, Meehan has seen a radical change in attitude about concussions in the years since he played sports as a teenager. When he was a young athlete, he and his teammates often laughed and joked about concussions and did not take them seriously. In fact, the word *concussion* was rarely used. "We got 'shaken up' or 'had our bells rung,'" he says. "We simply 'shook it off,' 'toughed it out,' or 'walked it off.' . . . Many times, we returned to the game in which we were injured. Often, we returned while still experiencing headaches, ringing in the ears, and other symptoms."[22]

In his book, *Kids, Sports, and Concussions*, Meehan describes a rugby game that took place during a time when concussions were believed to be minor injuries. The typical nonchalance about them was obvious in what happened after a player from Boston College was accidentally kicked in the head by an opponent. "As the ball was released," says Meehan, "he staggered away toward the wrong end of the field before collapsing to the ground. He rose unsteadily, only to collapse again. Finally, he rose to his feet and began sprinting, in an attempt to rejoin the play. But he was running in the wrong direction, away from ball. He fell one last time, only to be helped off of the field by his teammates." Meehan says that when the coach called out to ask what was wrong, one of the players yelled back that the young man was all right: "He just got his bell rung."[23]

All in the Head

Although research has heightened awareness of concussions and the associated problems, the injuries are not well understood by athletes, coaches, parents, and the general public. This is largely because concussions are not obvious like broken bones, severe lacerations, or other such injuries. As a result, they are often dismissed as not serious. In their book *The Concussion Crisis*, Linda Carroll and David Rosner write: "The inside joke among players and trainers depends on the belief that concussions are as harmless and transient as the cartoon stars floating around Sylvester the Cat's head every time he gets bonked. . . . It's hard to take seriously an invisible injury with subtle symptoms that often seem to pass quickly."[24]

Despite the fact that they are not obvious to outside observers, however, concussions are very real brain injuries. They result from damage to nerve cells (neurons) and disruptions in the brain's highly complex neurological circuitry. Inside the brain are hundreds of billions of neurons. Each contains a cell body as well as axons, which are long, threadlike "tails" that transmit messages from the brain to other parts of the body. Aided by chemical messengers known as neurotransmitters, the neurons in the

> " Although research has heightened awareness of concussions and the associated problems, the injuries are not well understood by athletes, coaches, parents, and the general public. "

brain work together in a way that is meticulously orchestrated, controlling how people think, feel, and act. When someone is concussed, this process is disrupted, as the Brain Injury Association of America writes:

> The stretching and squeezing of brain cells . . . can change the precise balance, which can result in problems in how the brain processes information. . . . Although the stretching and swelling of the axons may seem relatively minor or microscopic, the impact on the brain's neurological circuits can be significant. Even a "mild" injury can result in significant physiological damage and cognitive deficits.[25]

The neuronal dysfunction that is caused by a concussion can lead to significant changes in a sufferer's thoughts, feelings, and behaviors. Exactly what the effects are depends on which neurons have been damaged. For instance, someone may look dazed and forget where he or she is, but still be able to walk and talk normally. A college student named Nat wrote about his brother Jon sustaining a concussion while playing soccer:

> His eyes were unfocused, his legs would not bend, and he thought he was already sitting. He does not remember the actual injury or the moments that followed. We were later informed that his inability to control his body immediately following the [concussion] is common and fits the criteria of a temporary loss of brain function. His nervous system was still capable of walking and talking, but Jon himself was momentarily both unable to control his actions and unaware of them.[26]

A Youth Concussion Crisis

Many physicians who specialize in traumatic brain injury are concerned about what they perceive as a growing concussion problem among children and teenagers. Robert C. Cantu, who is one of the most well-known experts in the field, believes that there is an epidemic of youth concussions in the United States. He views this as a crisis because when young people sustain concussions, their symptoms are often more severe than those of adults, and their brains take longer to recover. Also, children's and adolescent's brains are not fully developed, which means they are more vulnerable to permanent, long-term damage from concussions. "Children are not adults," says Cantu. "Their bodies are still maturing. Their vulnerabilities to head trauma are far greater."[27]

Several recent studies have examined the prevalence of concussions among youth in the United States. One, released in April 2012, was conducted by a team of researchers from Children's Mercy Hospitals and Clinics in Kansas City, Missouri. Based on data accumulated by fourteen children's hospitals, the team determined that youth concussions diagnosed in emergency rooms nationwide more than doubled over a ten-year period: In 2001, 2,126 concussions were reported, and by 2010 that number had risen to 4,967.

> **The neuronal dysfunction that is caused by a concussion can lead to significant changes in a sufferer's thoughts, feelings, and behaviors.**

This appears to be an alarming finding, but the researchers say that it might actually be good news. Rather than indicating an increase in the number of brain injuries among youth, it could mean that concussions are more frequently reported and diagnosed than was the case a decade ago. If that is true, it is a sign that public education efforts to help prevent concussions have been working the way they are designed to work. Nevertheless, brain trauma experts remain concerned about the high number of concussions sustained by youth each year. Rosemarie Scolaro Moser, a neuropsychologist and concussion expert, writes: "In the past ten years, the number of eight- to thirteen-year-olds with a sports-related concussion has doubled, while the number of fourteen- to nineteen-year-olds seeking treatment for head injuries has increased by more than 200 percent."[28]

Post-Concussion Syndrome

Brain trauma experts say that an estimated 80 percent of people who sustain concussions will recover within seven to ten days, whereas the other 20 percent will need more time to heal. According to Cantu, between 5 and 10 percent of those will go on to develop post-concussion syndrome,

> **Brain trauma experts say that an estimated 80 percent of people who sustain concussions will recover within seven to ten days, whereas the other 20 percent will need more time to heal.**

in which symptoms last longer than a month. "Most of those with post-concussion syndrome will recover," says Cantu, "but some will take even over a year to recover and a very small number will never recover."[29]

Eighteen-year-old Sarah Parsons continues to suffer the effects of a concussion that happened during a high school junior varsity basketball game in 2009. While fighting for a rebound she landed on her head—and in that instant, her life changed dramatically. Her concussion was so severe that she had to miss four months of school. When she was finally able to return, she explains the rude awakening she faced:

I thought I could just go back to school and be the old Sarah again. Little did I know a part of that Sarah was gone, the teachers would be talking in class and I would have no idea what they were saying. I would try to focus and listen but I couldn't understand what most people said to me—it was like a foreign language. I would have to be told face to face and look at their mouth and still a good percentage of what they said I still didn't understand. I hurt every day; my head would throb, my left side of my body would be tingly, numb, and droopy. . . . Talking to people that were excited to see me back at school was embarrassing. I could hardly understand them and they didn't know. I couldn't tell them because I had a hard time saying coherent complete sentences.[30]

Today, even after so much time has passed, Parsons sometimes becomes depressed because she is not the same as she used to be. She still cannot go with her friends to movie theaters, amusement parks, or even the mall, because these sorts of places overstimulate her brain. There are days when she cannot drive a car. "Trust me," she says, "it has taken me time to accept my new life. Some days I still say 'what if?' Some days I still feel like poor me, I should have been doing this or that, and I get frustrated. But when I start feeling like that, I remember how blessed I am to be here." Parsons considers it a priority to share her experience with others in order to raise awareness of concussions, so she gives presentations to groups of coaches. "I am still the same Sarah Parsons I have always been," she says, "but now I have more to offer."[31]

Troops at Risk

Studies that focus on the military have consistently shown a high prevalence of concussions among troops who have served in combat zones. In the majority of cases, these concussions are caused by blasts from various forms of explosive devices. They may result from shock waves generated by roadside bombs, by the person's being thrown by the blast, or by shrapnel and other objects that fly through the air and hit the service member's body or head.

While the incidence of combat-related concussions is well established, what is not so widely known is the number of military personnel who sustain concussions before they ever get to active duty. According to an August 2012 report by ProPublica and NPR, thousands of troops sustain concussions each year during military training operations. The report cites a military study that focused on the Fort Hood US Army base in Texas, where almost 6 percent of soldiers who took hand-to-hand combat courses sustained concussions after being struck on the head. Although the study was relatively small, it sparked concern among brain trauma experts both inside and outside the military. If troops sustain concussions during training and are not treated before being deployed, they will be more vulnerable to the effects of additional concussions sustained while they are in combat zones.

> " While the incidence of combat-related concussions is well established, what is not so widely known is the number of military personnel who sustain concussions before they ever get to active duty. "

The military study revealed that most training-related concussions happen during sessions known as combatives. During basic training, all soldiers must take at least twenty-two hours of these courses, in which they learn fighting techniques drawn from martial arts, boxing, and wrestling. One of the early training routines, known as the "clinch and punch" drill, teaches defensive moves: One soldier throws a punch and another tries to avoid it by "clinching" the attacker's arms. But according to the military study, the "clinchers" do not always know how to properly defend themselves against the punches; as a result, they get hit repeatedly in the head.

According to retired US Army colonel and psychologist Harvey Watson, who was involved in the military study, the greatest risk is to female troops. They are typically much smaller than their male opponents and have the greatest incidence of training-related concussions. Watson explains: "I can tell you that it appears as if women in those kinds of drills become concussed—percentage wise—more often than men."[32] As a result of the study findings, military officials are working toward achieving a better balance between providing soldiers with proper training for combat while still ensuring their safety.

Not to Be Taken Lightly

Concussions are traumatic brain injuries that involve disruptions in neurological circuitry, which in turn affects how a sufferer thinks, feels, and acts. Much more is known about concussions today than in the past. For instance, studies have shown that youth are more vulnerable because their brains are not fully developed and because they can also take longer to recover from concussions. Research has also produced other findings, such as the high risk of concussions for military troops and the effects of post-concussion syndrome on those who develop it. As studies continue, scientists will inevitably learn more about concussions and their effects on sufferers.

What Are Concussions?

66 Some patients have suffered concussions in traffic accidents, mishaps around the house (they walked into a door), or a slip and fall in the grocery store.99

—Robert C. Cantu and Mark Hyman, *Concussions and Our Kids*. New York: Houghton Mifflin Harcourt, 2012.

Cantu is a Boston neurosurgeon and world-renowned expert on sports-related concussions, and Hyman is a sports journalist.

66 We are beginning to realize that young athletes are more susceptible to concussions than older ones.99

—David Geier, "Concussions in High School Athletes," Charleston Battery, June 14, 2012. www.charlestonbattery.com.

Geier is an orthopedic surgeon and director of the Medical University of South Carolina's Sports Medicine Program.

66 A more accurate term for a concussion is a brain injury rather than a head injury.99

—Don Brady and Flo Brady, "Sports-Related Concussions: Myths and Facts," National Association for School Psychologists *Communiqué Handout*, June 2011. www.concussiontreatment.com.

Don Brady is a clinical and school psychologist, and Flo Brady is a child and family services counselor.

* Editor's Note: While the definition of a primary source can be narrowly or broadly defined, for the purposes of Compact Research, a primary source consists of: 1) results of original research presented by an organization or researcher; 2) eyewitness accounts of events, personal experience, or work experience; 3) first-person editorials offering pundits' opinions; 4) government officials presenting political plans and/or policies; 5) representatives of organizations presenting testimony or policy.

66 **A concussion results from a closed-head type of injury and does not include injuries in which there is bleeding under the skull or into the brain.** 99

—John P. Cunha, "Concussion," eMedicineHealth, July 18, 2011. www.emedicinehealth.com.

Cunha is an emergency medicine physician at Holy Cross Hospital in Fort Lauderdale, Florida.

66 **While temporary loss of consciousness due to injury means that a concussion has taken place, most concussions occur without the patient being knocked out.** 99

—Benjamin Wedro, "Concussion," MedicineNet, August 27, 2012. www.medicinenet.com.

Wedro is an emergency medicine physician at Gundersen Clinic, a regional trauma center in La Crosse, Wisconsin.

66 **Concussions are a significant threat to our nation's youth, particularly those participating in sports.** 99

—Vikas Kapil, "Protecting School-Age Athletes from Sports-Related Concussion Injury," CDC congressional testimony, September 8, 2010. www.cdc.gov.

Kapil is an emergency medicine and public health physician.

66 **Studies have consistently demonstrated that, with the exception of cheerleading, concussions are more likely to occur during competition than during practice.** 99

—William Paul Meehan III, *Kids, Sports, and Concussions*. Santa Barbara, CA: ABC-CLIO, 2011.

Meehan is director of the Sports Concussion Clinic in the Division of Sports Medicine at Boston Children's Hospital.

❝It is a common misconception that concussion is a problem seen only in males. Concussions occur in females as well, with some data suggesting that concussion incidence is higher in females when compared to males playing similar sports.❞

—Jeffrey Kutcher, testimony before the US Senate Committee on Commerce, Science, and Transportation, October 19, 2011. www.aan.com.

Kutcher is chief of inpatient neurological services at the University of Michigan Health System and chair of the American Academy of Neurology's Sports Neurology section.

....

❝The signs and symptoms of a concussion can be difficult to sort out. Early on, problems may be missed by the person with the concussion, family members, or doctors.❞

—CDC, *Facts About Concussion and Brain Injury*, 2010. www.cdc.gov.

The CDC is dedicated to protecting health and promoting quality of life through the prevention and control of disease, injury, and disability.

....

What Are Concussions?

- According to the CDC, children from **birth to four** years, adolescents aged **fifteen to nineteen** years, and adults aged **sixty-five and older** are most likely to sustain a concussion.

- The Center for Injury Research and Policy in Columbus, Ohio, states that in 2010 more high school **soccer players** sustained concussions than did athletes in basketball, baseball, wrestling, and softball combined.

- According to a study published in May 2012 by the Trust for America's Health and the Robert Wood Johnson Foundation, the most common cause of traumatic brain injury, including concussions, is **accidental falls**.

- According to neurosurgeon and concussion expert Richard G. Ellenbogen, the number one cause of concussions in the United States is **wheel sports**, such as cycling, followed by football, playground injuries, running and falling, and soccer (in that order).

- A study published in September 2010 in the medical journal *Pediatrics* found that between 1997 and 2007, concussion-related visits to emergency rooms **doubled** for children aged eight to thirteen and **tripled** for adolescents aged fourteen to nineteen.

- According to data compiled by the National Collegiate Athletic Association, the highest rate of reported concussions in college sports is in **women's ice hockey**, with nearly twice as many concussions per 1,000 players as occur in men's ice hockey.

Football, Girls' Soccer Have Highest Concussion Rates

To better understand the prevalence of concussions among high school athletes, a team of researchers from Columbus, Ohio, conducted a study and published the results in April 2012. They found that football had the highest number of concussions, followed by girls' soccer and boys' wrestling.

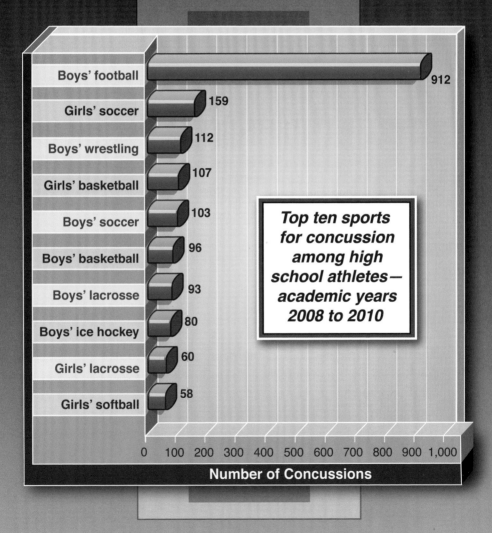

Top ten sports for concussion among high school athletes—academic years 2008 to 2010

Source: Mallika Marar et al. "Epidemiology of Concussions Among United States High School Athletes in 20 Sports," *American Journal of Sports Medicine*, April 2012. www.udel.edu.

Concussion Symptoms

According to the Centers for Disease Control and Prevention, symptoms that an individual has sustained a concussion usually fall into four categories: thinking/remembering, physical, emotional/mood, and sleep.

Thinking/ Remembering	Physical	Emotional/ Mood	Sleep
Difficulty thinking clearly	Headache Fuzzy or blurred vision	Irritability	Sleeping more than usual
Feeling slowed down	Nausea or vomiting (early on) Dizziness	Sadness	Sleeping less than usual
Difficulty concentrating	Sensitivity to noise or light Balance problems	More emotional than usual	Trouble falling asleep
Difficulty remembering new information	Feeling tired, having no energy	Nervousness or anxiety	

Source: Centers for Disease Control and Prevention, "Concussion," March 8, 2010. www.cdc.gov.

- The CDC estimates that the number of sports- and recreation-related concussion visits to emergency rooms increased **62 percent** between 2001 and 2009.

- A study published in May 2012 by the Trust for America's Health and the Robert Wood Johnson Foundation found that children and teens between the ages of ten and nineteen account for more than **70 percent** of concussion-related visits to emergency rooms due to sports and recreational activities.

Concussion Causes Vary by Age

In August 2012 the American Osteopathic Association surveyed 1,303 adults over the age of eighteen to learn in what activities they had been involved when they experienced a concussion. As this graph shows, young adults were more apt to sustain concussions while playing sports, whereas among the oldest group the main cause was accidents away from the home.

How respondents sustained concussions by age group:

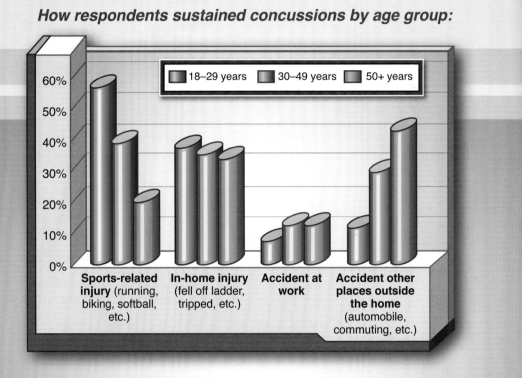

Note: Totals exceed 100 percent because some respondents sustained more than one concussion.

Source: American Osteopathic Association, "2012 Concussion Survey: Final Results," September 2012, p. 11.

- According to the American Association of Neurological Surgeons, between **50 and 70 percent** of concussions are the result of a motor vehicle crash.

How Are Concussions Diagnosed and Treated?

66What makes the diagnosis and treatment of concussions especially tough is that people can't see brain injuries with the naked eye like they can a sprained ankle.99

—Ken Reed, a physician and sports policy director for the sports reform organization League of Fans.

66The frustration is that there is zero treatment for concussion. We have nothing that completely eliminates symptoms.99

—Charles H. Tator, a neurosurgeon and concussion expert from Toronto, Canada.

Amy Garry, a ten-year-old girl from Yardley, Pennsylvania, loves to play soccer. So when she sustained a concussion during a match in August 2012, being told that she had to stay away from her beloved sport did not make her happy. Amy was diagnosed by neuropsychologist Rosemarie Scolaro Moser, who prescribed a regimen of physical and cognitive rest. That meant no exercise of any kind, as well as no television, reading, computer use, or even playing with her friends. Amy's mother, Rachel Garry, was concerned about such strict requirements and did not want her daughter to feel like she was being punished for getting injured. She explains: "For a 10-year-old who's usually running around—she was supposed to go to soccer camp with her team this week—it's really hard."[33]

After the period of rest was over, though, Rachel knew that the doctor had been right. Taking the prescribed time off cured Amy's headaches and alleviated other symptoms of the concussion as well. "Amy seems more like herself," says Rachel. "She's a very bright, bubbly girl and wasn't [before seeing] Dr. Moser. Just these last two days, she's laughing and not complaining of headaches. It's really remarkable—just from the rest."[34]

Diagnostic Challenges

According to Moser, in too many cases athletes are not properly evaluated when a concussion is suspected, which can cause serious problems. In fact, it is not uncommon for coaches to rely on what the athlete says when asked if he or she feels up to returning to the game. Unfortunately, children and teens often do not know how to identify concussion symptoms in themselves, nor do they understand the long-term consequences of concussions. Moser cites a study of more than fifteen hundred high school students that found more than 66 percent of those who had sustained a concussion did not think their symptoms were serious enough to report. The same study found that 41 percent of athletes who suspected they had been concussed refrained from telling anyone because they did not want to leave the game.

The reluctance to admit concussion symptoms is extremely common among athletes of all ages, who would rather hide the fact that they are hurt than not be able to participate in their sport. National Association for Stock Car Auto Racing (NASCAR) driver Jeff Gordon admits this is true of him. After fellow driver Dale Earnhardt Jr. was praised for having the courage to seek medical attention for a concussion and miss a championship race, Gordon said that he would not have done the same thing:

> Honestly, I hate to say this, but no, I wouldn't. If I have a shot at the championship, there's two races to go, my head is hurting, and I just came through a wreck, and I am feeling signs of it, but I'm still leading the points, or second in the points, I'm not going to say anything. I'm sorry. You know, that's the competitor in me. . . . That's not the way it should be. It's something that most of us, I think, would do. I think that's what gets a lot of us in trouble.[35]

One of the most difficult aspects of diagnosing concussions, even for physicians, is the lack of any sort of laboratory test that can confirm the diagnosis. Health-care professionals must rely on their own judgment when evaluating the patient and make an evaluation based on systems such as balance problems, headache, blurred vision, and dizziness, among others. This can be difficult because there are no specific guidelines, nor do any two people exhibit the exact same symptoms. Sports medicine specialist William Oates explains: "Every mind is wired differently and, therefore, the presence or absence of concussion symptoms varies greatly from athlete to athlete. For this reason, great time and care must be taken when evaluating the severity of an athlete's concussion, especially because symptoms are often subtle."[36]

Baseline Testing

A growing number of schools and athletic organizations are addressing the challenge of identifying concussions by implementing baseline testing programs. In general terms, *baseline* refers to a starting point from which comparisons can be made, and this is the underlying concept of baseline concussion testing. At the start of a sports season, before athletes have had exposure to practices or competition, they undergo a series of computerized neurological tests. The tests are designed to measure the athletes' cognitive abilities and set a baseline for gauging each individual's brain function. If an athlete is suspected of being concussed, he or she takes the same test again, and the two scores are compared. Professional NASCAR driver Steve Park, who has sustained several concussions and is a strong supporter of baseline testing, explains: "Say your personal score is 1500 (before injury). That goes in your record. Now afterwards, if you have a head injury and come back and take the test and score a 350 . . . they can look at where you were not doing well and say, 'This is what's impaired.'"[37]

> " The reluctance to admit concussion symptoms is extremely common among athletes of all ages, who would rather hide the fact that they are hurt than not be able to participate in their sport. "

The leading baseline testing product is called ImPACT, which stands for Immediate Post-Concussion Assessment and Cognitive Testing. It was developed in the 1990s by Mark Lovell, a neuropsychologist who directs the Center for Sports Medicine Concussion Program at the University of Pittsburgh, and neurosurgeon Joseph Maroon. The ImPACT test takes less than half an hour and measures memory, reaction time, mental speed, information processing, and other brain functions that are typically affected by concussions. According to Lovell, one important benefit of this testing method is that diagnoses are made based on actual data, rather than on what the athletes say about themselves. He explains:

> A growing number of schools and athletic organizations are addressing the challenge of identifying concussions by implementing baseline testing programs.

> Before we had tests like ImPACT, a lot of it came down to what the athlete told you. You'd ask: "Do you have a headache? Do you feel nauseous? Do you feel dizzy?" They generally say no to all of those. . . . One thing we know about athletes is they're very, very competitive. So we weren't absolutely positive we were always being given an accurate picture of how they were feeling. With a test like ImPACT, you can't cheat it.[38]

The Healing Power of Rest

When someone has sustained a concussion, a physician can treat headache symptoms by prescribing medication. But the brain heals on its own, and there is nothing doctors can do to facilitate that healing process or speed it up. The only option is complete and total rest, both cognitive and physical. Neuropsychologist Gerald Tramontano writes: "This allows the brain to devote all its resources to healing." He goes on to say that in order for the brain to fully recover from a concussion, it must "quickly reorganize itself and enlist other neurons to take over the work of those that have been damaged."[39]

This healing process is often complete within a week or two after the concussion has occurred. It may, however, take weeks, months, or even longer, depending on the individual and the severity of the concussion. Tramontano emphasizes how crucial it is for the patient to spend ample time resting, yet he acknowledges that it can be difficult to know how long is long enough. "How can you tell how much rest is needed?" he asks. "It's not enough to simply wait until the 'fog clears' or even have the athlete take a cautionary week or two off." According to Tramontano, this is another reason why baseline testing is so valuable, as he writes: "The only way to know for sure whether a concussion victim's brain has returned to normal is to compare the results of neuropsychological tests conducted before and after the injury. . . . Because the tests can remove the guesswork in determining whether someone is ready to return to the field, they are an essential part of protective equipment for athletes."[40]

> " Concussion specialists have known for years that rest is necessary to facilitate the brain's healing after a concussion, but this was not supported by scientific research. "

A Revealing Study

Concussion specialists have known for years that rest is necessary to facilitate the brain's healing after a concussion, but this treatment had not been supported by scientific research. That changed in 2012 with the publication of a study by Moser and her colleagues at the Sports Concussion Center of New Jersey. Conducted between April 2010 and September 2011, the study involved forty-nine high school–age and college-age athletes. All had sustained concussions at various times and had sought treatment for symptoms such as recurrent headaches and trouble concentrating. Participants were assigned to groups based on the amount of time that had passed following the concussion: a week or less, a month, or between one and seven months. Each individual underwent baseline tests that measured memory, processing speed, and reaction time. Then all were ordered to rest for a full week, meaning they could not go to school or work, exercise, watch television, read, socialize (including texting or talking on the phone), or use a computer.

At the conclusion of the study, participants were again given the baseline tests, and in every case their scores had improved dramatically. This was true regardless of the time that had elapsed between their concussion and the onset of the resting period. According to Moser, the study proves what concussion specialists have long known—that rest is the answer to helping the brain heal itself after a concussion. She explains: "Our research now provides clinicians with solid evidence to show athletes, parents, schools and teams that rest really helps and should not be underestimated, no matter how long the time from injury. I hope it helps us debunk the mistaken philosophy that it is better to push through the pain, than to take the time to heal."[41]

A Holistic Approach

Sadness, irritability, and depression are common among young people who have sustained concussions, especially those whose symptoms linger for a long time. This was the case with eleven-year-old Cole Barrett, who suffered a concussion in 2011 when a ball slammed into the side of his helmet during a lacrosse game. When Cole was diagnosed with a concussion, his parents expected that it would take time for his headaches and other symptoms to subside. What they were not prepared for, however, was that their son would have such a radical change in personality that he seemed like a totally different person. "The psycho-social part, it can creep up on you at any point in time," says his mother, Bernadette. "At first, you think everything's OK, but then you've got yelling, screaming and crying and don't know where it's coming from."[42]

Cole continued to feel depressed and anxious, which caused his stress level to escalate and his mood swings to become more severe. Also, whenever the subject of school was brought up,

> " Sadness, irritability, and depression are common among young people who have sustained concussions, especially those whose symptoms linger for a long time. "

his headaches got worse because he was worried about getting behind in his assignments. His parents took him to Children's Hospital Colorado, where he was seen by Michael Dichiaro, a physician who works with youth who have concussions. Dichiaro evaluated Cole and developed a holistic treatment program for him, meaning one that was designed to treat the mind as well as the body. Along with a period of rest, Cole's treatment involved psychotherapy and pain-management techniques such as biofeedback, relaxation, and breathing exercises.

Cole made excellent progress in his recovery, and by the end of the program he felt better physically as well as emotionally. He returned to school, starting with half days and gradually working up to full-time, and his grades bounced back to where they were before the concussion. To his parents' relief, Cole's emotional problems have cleared up, and he has even expressed interest in playing lacrosse again, which is a huge change from his state of mind after being injured. "He turned the corner on school," Bernadette says. "Now he's got to turn the corner on athletics. Just this week he mentioned that he was interested in joining a team."[43]

Hurdles and Hope

Even though concussions are common injuries, they remain challenging to diagnose and treat. Unlike other types of injuries, there are no laboratory tests or scans that can confirm or rule out concussions; physicians must make assessments based on the patient's symptoms. Nor are there treatments that can help people recover from concussions, other than periods of complete rest so the brain can heal itself. As scientists continue to explore the mysteries of the human brain and learn more about concussions, these challenges will hopefully be overcome.

How Are Concussions Diagnosed and Treated?

66 **Children, in particular might not exhibit the first symptoms until *days* after a particularly hard hit or rough tackle, which makes diagnosing a concussion not only difficult but often impossible—even for a trained specialist.** 99

—Rosemarie Scolaro Moser, *Ahead of the Game*. Lebanon, NH: University Press of New England, 2012.

Moser is a neuropsychologist and rehabilitation specialist who has been treating and researching concussion for more than twenty-five years.

66 **It is understandably frustrating for doctors, parents, coaches, and athletes that no medical test can definitively diagnose a concussion.** 99

—William Paul Meehan III, *Kids, Sports, and Concussions*. Santa Barbara, CA: ABC-CLIO, 2011.

Meehan is director of the Sports Concussion Clinic in the Division of Sports Medicine at Boston Children's Hospital.

* Editor's Note: While the definition of a primary source can be narrowly or broadly defined, for the purposes of Compact Research, a primary source consists of: 1) results of original research presented by an organization or researcher; 2) eyewitness accounts of events, personal experience, or work experience; 3) first-person editorials offering pundits' opinions; 4) government officials presenting political plans and/or policies; 5) representatives of organizations presenting testimony or policy.

Primary Source Quotes

> **Currently there are no specific drugs for the treatment or prevention of concussions and the long term effects of concussions.**

—Bennet Omalu, "Head and Other Injuries in Youth, High School, College and Professional Football," oral statement at the US Congress judiciary forum, February 1, 2010. www.braininjuryresearchinstitute.org.

Omalu is a neuropathologist and codirector of the Brain Injury Research Institute at West Virginia University.

> **Rest is the hallmark of concussion therapy. The best we can do for patients is to shut things down physically and cognitively.**

—Robert C. Cantu and Mark Hyman, *Concussions and Our Kids*. New York: Houghton Mifflin Harcourt, 2012.

Cantu is a Boston neurosurgeon and world-renowned expert on concussions, and Hyman is a sports journalist.

> **Unfortunately, many years passed in which concussions were not diagnosed and managed as they are today.**

—Mandy Huggins, "NFL Concussion Litigation: A Doctor's Perspective," *Ruling Sports* (blog), July 30, 2012. http://rulingsports.com.

Huggins is a sports medicine physician from South Florida.

> **Concussion can be an easy diagnosis when the athlete gets knocked out on the field or is slow to get up, but often, concussions are subtle and even the athlete isn't aware that the brain has been shaken.**

—Benjamin Wedro, "Concussion," MedicineNet, August 27, 2012. www.medicinenet.com.

Wedro is an emergency medicine physician at Gundersen Clinic, a regional trauma center in La Crosse, Wisconsin.

> **Concussion cannot be diagnosed by any one test. It is a diagnosis that can only be made by a careful clinical evaluation performed by a health care professional, and preferably one with training and experience caring for brain injuries.**

—Jeffrey Kutcher, testimony before the US Senate Committee on Commerce, Science, and Transportation, October 19, 2011. www.aan.com.

Kutcher is chief of inpatient neurological services at the University of Michigan Health System and chair of the American Academy of Neurology's Sports Neurology section.

> **Most people with a concussion recover quickly and fully.**

—Vikas Kapil, "Protecting School-Age Athletes from Sports-Related Concussion Injury," CDC congressional testimony, September 8, 2010. www.cdc.gov.

Kapil is an emergency medicine and public health physician.

> **In more severe cases of postconcussion syndrome, cognitive behavioral therapy (a type of psychological therapy) may be helpful.**

—Ryszard M. Pluta, "Concussion," *Journal of the American Medical Association*, July 6, 2011. http://jama.jamanetwork.com.

Pluta is a physician with the National Institute of Neurological Disorders and Stroke.

> **It [is] imperative that we focus on early recognition and diagnosis of concussion injuries, especially in our children, who depend on us for their safety.**

—Lyle J. Micheli, foreword to *Kids, Sports, and Concussions*, by William Paul Meehan III. Santa Barbara, CA: ABC-CLIO, 2011.

Micheli is director of the Division of Sports Medicine at Boston Children's Hospital.

Facts and Illustrations

How Are Concussions
Diagnosed and Treated?

- According to neuropsychologist and concussion expert Rosemarie Scolaro Moser, studies of high school students have shown that athletes who were **allowed to rest** after sustaining a concussion recovered **twice as quickly** as those who were not.

- **CT and/or MRI scans** are often recommended after a serious head blow to detect skull fracture, brain swelling, or bleeding, but brain trauma experts say that these tests cannot detect most concussions.

- According to the CDC, one of the **challenges** of diagnosing concussions is that symptoms resemble those of other medical conditions such as post-traumatic stress disorder, depression, and headache syndromes.

- According to David Allen Hovda, director of the University of California–Los Angeles Brain Injury Research Center, about **80 percent** of people who suffer concussions recover in less than fourteen days if they avoid additional bumps or jolts to the head.

- The American Association of Neurological Surgeons says that postconcussion headaches may be treated with acetaminophen (Tylenol) but are often **resistant to stronger, narcotic-based pain medications**.

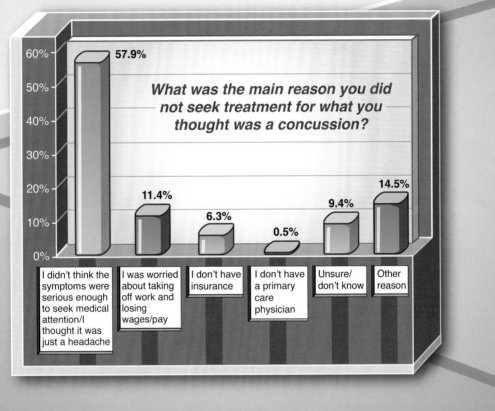

Reasons Adults Do Not Seek Treatment for Concussions

In a 2012 survey by the American Osteopathic Association, participants who thought they had sustained a concussion but did not seek treatment were asked to share their reasons. As this graph shows, most did not think their symptoms were serious enough.

What was the main reason you did not seek treatment for what you thought was a concussion?

57.9% — I didn't think the symptoms were serious enough to seek medical attention/I thought it was just a headache

11.4% — I was worried about taking off work and losing wages/pay

6.3% — I don't have insurance

0.5% — I don't have a primary care physician

9.4% — Unsure/don't know

14.5% — Other reason

Source: American Osteopathic Association, "2012 Concussion Survey: Final Results," September 2012. p. 11.

- According to physician and brain trauma expert William Paul Meehan III, medical research is underway at Boston Children's Hospital to develop tests that could potentially diagnose a concussion using **blood, urine, or cerebral spinal fluid.**

Concussion Screening Lax Among Troops Exposed to Bomb Blasts

Military studies have found that a leading cause of concussions among troops stationed in combat zones is exposure to bomb blasts. Screening for such injuries is crucial so that sufferers can be promptly diagnosed and treated—but according to a survey published in February 2011, the vast majority of troops who were exposed to bomb blasts in Afghanistan during 2010 were not examined for concussions.

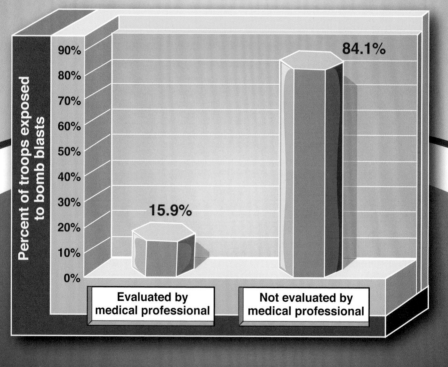

Source: Joint Mental Health Advisory Team 7, "Operation Enduring Freedom 2010 Afghanistan," February 22, 2011. www.armymedicine.army.mil.

- The Sports Concussion Institute cites a survey in which only **68 percent** of chief resident physicians said they felt comfortable managing sport-related concussions.

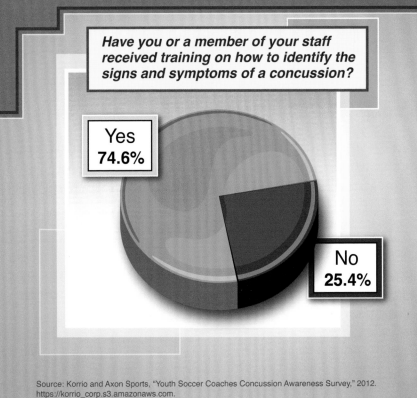

Most Youth Soccer Coaches Trained in Identifying Concussions

To gain insight into concussion awareness and training among US youth soccer coaches, the athletic companies Korrio and Axon Sports conducted a survey during November and December 2011. One finding was that three-fourths of the coaches (or a staff member) had been trained in how to identify concussions in athletes.

Have you or a member of your staff received training on how to identify the signs and symptoms of a concussion?

Yes
74.6%

No
25.4%

Source: Korrio and Axon Sports, "Youth Soccer Coaches Concussion Awareness Survey," 2012. https://korrio_corp.s3.amazonaws.com.

- According to sports medicine physician Andrew Blecher, supplements such as **omega 3 fatty acids** may be of benefit to brain function and concussion recovery, although this has not been scientifically proved.

- According to the Sports Concussion Institute, a history of **developmental or psychiatric disorders** or a history of **migraine headaches** can have an effect on concussion recovery time.

What Are the Risks of Concussions?

> **A growing body of research has recently uncovered truths about concussion that scientists never before understood, and the findings have been nothing short of terrifying.**
>
> —Rosemarie Scolaro Moser, a neuropsychologist and rehabilitation specialist who has been treating and researching concussion for more than twenty-five years.

> **No one understands how important the brain is until you injure it. It's not an easy life to live when you have a concussion.**
>
> —Michael Collins, executive director of the University of Pittsburgh Medical Center for Sports Medicine and a noted expert on concussions.

In February 2012, while playing soccer with a group of his fellow graduate students, journalist Dan Keane was hit in the face with the ball. The impact knocked him backward and made him dizzy enough that he lay down on the field to stop his head from spinning. When he got up and made his way over to the bench to sit down, Keane says he was overcome with "a bottomless sadness" that was unlike anything he had ever felt before. He writes: "The feeling seemed to arise directly from the confusion of my initial dizziness. . . . I felt detached from the game, and from life, like I was watching my life from the outside. And then the feeling just got very, very sad. Tired and sad. Exhausted. Defeated."[44]

Overpowering Sadness

Keane went to the emergency room, where he was examined and diagnosed with what doctors called a "mild concussion." When he described the unbearable sadness that had swept over him, he was told that it was a common symptom. The doctors informed him that the problems he was having would clear up within seven to ten days—yet three months later he was still plagued by a near-constant state of gloom and a number of frustrating problems. He suffered from constant headaches. He says he had trouble with memory, sometimes fumbling to find the right words, "drawing a blank on a classmate's name, throwing the crosswords down when they started spinning."
He was exhausted all the time and found that he could not write. His despair became so overpowering that one night, as his head was aching unbearably, he "sat on the couch at a party among friends and told myself that I wanted to die."[45]

> " The greatest long-term risk is for those who sustain multiple concussions and do not allow their brains to heal properly after being injured. "

By June 2012, four months after his concussion, Keane finally started to see improvement. The sadness had lifted, he had more energy, and the cognitive issues were resolved. Even today, however, he is reminded every so often that he sustained a serious brain injury. "I do notice with some dismay that pale, shadowy versions of the concussion headache will still creep up when I'm really tired," he says. He feels as though he is healed emotionally and cognitively, but has some doubt about that because of how badly the concussion frightened him. "This is one of the creepy things about a concussion for neurotic types like me," he says. "Am I really fine? Or is my brain now permanently a step slower, and I just can't tell?"[46]

A Downward Slide

Keane's months-long struggle with the effects of his concussion is not common. Brain trauma experts say that symptoms typically fade within a week or two for at least 80 percent of people who are concussed. The greatest long-term risk is for those who sustain multiple concussions and do not allow their brains to heal properly after being injured. They risk causing irreversible damage to the brain, which is what happened to race car driver Jeff Vochaska. Throughout a career that spanned more than thirty years, Vochaska won a record-breaking 116 races. As is characteristic of racing, he was involved in innumerable car crashes over that time—and in the process he suffered as many as seventy concussions. This has taken a heavy toll on his brain and his quality of life. "I'll never be able to be normal," he says. "I spend most of my time sitting here in the living room, I have drapes that block out all of the light, I can't stand bright lights. I can't stand noises. I sit here in the living room in the dark most of the time."[47]

In a 2012 interview, Vochaska spoke candidly about the brain damage from years of racing-related crashes. He now realizes there were warning signs along the way, but he did not know they were symptoms of concussion. After a serious wreck, for instance, he often felt like he had a case of stomach flu. As time went by the symptoms grew more pronounced and lasted longer, as he explains: "Originally it was only two or three days, but then it got to the point where I would be sick for a couple of weeks. I then finally got to the point a couple of years ago where the symptoms just never went away."[48]

Vochaska says he finally realized the seriousness of his condition after a terrible wreck that occurred in 2010. "I remember getting out of the car and the safety crew was talking to me, but I couldn't hear them," he says. "After that I was always sick." Since that time his health has continued to deteriorate and he feels a growing sense of despair over what has happened to him. "I used to be outgoing and happy," he says, "and now I have a hard time talking to people."[49]

Second-Impact Syndrome

When athletes sustain a concussion, it is essential that they not return to play before their brain is fully healed. If they get back in the game too soon, they risk developing a rare but catastrophic condition known as second-impact syndrome. This occurs because the brain is much more vulnerable to injury after it has already been injured, and it only takes minimal force to cause damage that is severe and irreversible. Terry Zeigler, a certified athletic trainer who specializes in the prevention, treatment, and rehabilitation of injuries, writes: "The athlete does not need to receive a strong second blow to the head to set the effects in motion. The athlete may receive only a minor blow to the head or a hit to the chest or back that snaps the head enough to have the brain rebound inside the skull."[50] If that happens, the brain swells rapidly, and death can occur within minutes.

Second-impact syndrome was originally identified by neurosurgeon Robert E. Harbaugh and neurologist Richard L. Saunders, who gave the disorder its name in an article published in 1984. The subject of their article was the tragic death of Enzo Montemurro, a nineteen-year-old football player from Cornell University. During an October 1981 game with Dartmouth, Montemurro bumped into an opposing player and immediately collapsed on the field. Officials rushed to his aid but found Montemurro unresponsive, and he was rushed by ambulance to the hospital. A CT scan showed extensive swelling in his brain, and although doctors worked frantically to save him, the young man died.

> " **The brain is much more vulnerable to injury after it has already been injured, and it only takes minimal force to cause damage that is severe and irreversible.** "

In a follow-up investigation, officials discovered that Montemurro had been punched in the head during a fistfight four days before the game. He was diagnosed with a concussion and advised to avoid any contact sports until his symptoms resolved. He did not listen, however, and asked for medical clearance to play, insisting that his headaches were gone—a decision that cost him his life. In their book, *The Concussion Crisis*, Linda Carroll and David Rosner write:

> The warning was clear: second-impact syndrome could occur any time an athlete suffered a jolt to the head too close on the heels of an earlier concussion. If the brain didn't have enough time to recover from the initial concussion, a second one could have a much more devastating impact—even when the second resulted from noth-

ing more than a light tap. That second hit could cause the brain to swell catastrophically. But it was the first hit, Saunders and Harbaugh discovered, that had made the player into a walking time bomb.[51]

Slow Destruction of the Brain

One of the most catastrophic results of repeated blows to the head is a condition known as chronic traumatic encephalopathy, or CTE. It is a progressive, degenerative brain disease that affects those who have a history of repeated brain trauma. The cumulative trauma triggers an abnormal buildup of a protein called tau in the brain, as *Time* magazine senior editor Jeffrey Kluger writes: "The protein is one of the major structural materials of nerve tissues. When the brain is shaken too hard, nerve fibers are torn and the tau is released. The brain tries to clean up the mess, and given enough time, it could. If the hits keep coming, however, the proteins just accumulate."[52] As tau continues to build up, it destroys cells throughout the brain, including those that regulate impulse control, judgment, emotions, and memory.

> **One of the most catastrophic results of repeated blows to the head is a condition known as chronic traumatic encephalopathy, or CTE.**

CTE was first discovered in September 2002 by a neuropathologist named Bennet Omalu. He was performing an autopsy on the body of retired pro football player Mike Webster, who had died of a heart attack at age fifty. Omalu was born and raised in the African country of Nigeria and did not understand the American obsession with football. He did know that it was a violent sport with an extremely high concussion rate, especially for men like Webster who played professionally. He had heard reports of how Webster's personality had changed dramatically after his retirement from pro football, and that he had been exhibiting bizarre behavior for over a decade. Omalu wondered: "How did this big athletic man end up so crazy in the head?"[53]

Omalu was reminded of a disorder that was identified in 1928 called dementia pugilistica. Also known as "punch-drunk syndrome," it affected boxers who had been punched in the head so many times that their brains severely deteriorated. It made sense to Omalu that if repeated blows to the head could destroy the brains of boxers, the same could happen to football players who were hit multiple times throughout their careers. He knew the condition could be diagnosed only after someone had died, but his initial examination of Webster's brain found no abnormalities. So, Omalu was granted permission to perform a microscopic analysis of brain tissue. He was shocked at what he discovered—brownish-red splotches, which he knew was a heavy accumulation of the tau protein. Journalist and author Jeanne Marie Laskas writes: "Tau was kind of like sludge, clogging up the works, killing cells in regions responsible for mood, emotions, and executive functioning. This was why Mike Webster was crazy."[54] Omalu named the disorder chronic traumatic encephalopathy (CTE) and published several papers about his finding.

> " **CTE has been found in at least a dozen deceased veterans who have served in combat zones and sustained multiple concussions.** "

In the years since Omalu's discovery, he and other researchers have examined the brains of more than one hundred deceased professional and amateur athletes. They have found CTE in a disturbing number of them—including Nathan Stiles, who was only seventeen years old when he collapsed and died during a football game in 2010. His brain was examined by Boston neuropathologist Ann McKee, who was shocked to find CTE in someone so young.

A Tragic End

CTE is typically associated with those who are involved in hard-hitting collision sports, but it is not limited to athletes. Soon after Omalu identified the condition, he began thinking about veterans who had served in combat zones and suffered from repeated blast-related concussions. They were often diagnosed with post-traumatic stress disorder, but Omalu's theory was that they could actually be suffering from CTE. He and his colleagues at the Brain Injury Research Institute expanded their investigations to include deceased veterans.

In November 2011 Omalu coauthored an article in which he discussed finding CTE in a twenty-seven-year-old former US marine. The young man, whose name was Michael Smith, had been honorably discharged from the military in 2009 after two tours in Iraq. Not long after arriving home, his life began to spiral out of control. He developed severe memory problems, had horrifying nightmares, and was angry much of the time. He struggled with alcohol abuse and got into a drunk-driving crash that cost him his driver's license. In 2010, eight months after leaving the military, he killed himself. When Omalu examined Smith's brain, he discovered that it had been ravaged by CTE. Since that discovery, CTE has been found in at least a dozen other deceased veterans who have served in combat zones and sustained multiple concussions.

Handle Brain with Care

Most people who are concussed recover within a relatively short time with no residual effects. But because concussions are brain injuries, there is always a risk of more serious problems. Lingering headaches and memory loss can cause depression and feelings of hopelessness, while cumulative damage from multiple concussions can seriously impair quality of life. In the worst cases, the brain can literally waste away from the devastating disease known as CTE. As awareness of these and other risks continues to grow, the public will hopefully realize that concussions must be taken seriously.

What Are the Risks of Concussions?

66 **There is not enough valid, reliable or objective scientific evidence at present to determine whether or not repeat head impacts in professional football result in long term brain damage.** 99

—Ira Casson, testimony to the US House Judiciary Committee, January 4, 2010. http://judiciary.house.gov.

Casson is a neurologist from New York and former cochair of the NFL's panel on head injuries.

66 **We have known about concussions and the effects of concussions in football for over a century. Every blow to the head is dangerous. Repeated concussions and sub-concussions both have the capacity to cause permanent brain damage.** 99

—Bennet Omalu, "Head and Other Injuries in Youth, High School, College and Professional Football," oral statement at the US Congress judiciary forum, February 1, 2010. www.braininjuryresearchinstitute.org.

Omalu is a neuropathologist and codirector of the Brain Injury Research Institute at West Virginia University.

Primary Source Quotes

"All injuries to the brain are potentially serious and devastating."

—Benjamin Wedro, "Concussion," MedicineNet, August 27, 2012. www.medicinenet.com.

Wedro is an emergency medicine physician at Gundersen Clinic, a regional trauma center in La Crosse, Wisconsin.

"If people attempt to play through a brain or spinal cord injury, they do so at great personal peril. It can be fatal."

—Hunt Batjer, "House Call: The Dangers of Concussion in the Young," *San Angelo (TX) Standard-Times*, December 12, 2011. www.gosanangelo.com.

Batjer is chair of the Department of Neurological Surgery at Northwestern University Feinberg School of Medicine in Chicago.

"In rare cases, repeat concussion can result in brain swelling, permanent brain damage, and even death."

—Vikas Kapil, "Protecting School-Age Athletes from Sports-Related Concussion Injury," CDC congressional testimony, September 8, 2010. www.cdc.gov.

Kapil is an emergency medicine and public health physician.

"If not recognized and treated early on, repeated injuries to the brain can result in lasting and permanent damage."

—Lyle J. Micheli, foreword to *Kids, Sports, and Concussions*, by William Paul Meehan III. Santa Barbara, CA: ABC-CLIO, 2011.

Micheli is director of the Division of Sports Medicine at Boston Children's Hospital.

66 Older adults may have a higher risk of serious complications from a concussion, such as bleeding on the brain. 99

—CDC, *Facts About Concussion and Brain Injury*, 2010. www.cdc.gov.

The CDC is dedicated to protecting health and promoting quality of life through the prevention and control of disease, injury, and disability.

66 Concussion in children . . . can pose serious health risks, ranging from temporary memory lapses to fatal brain swelling. 99

—Sherilyn W. Driscoll, "Concussion in Children: What Are the Effects?," Mayo Clinic, May 19, 2012. www.mayoclinic.com.

Driscoll is a pediatric and adolescent medicine specialist with the Mayo Clinic.

66 Even mild concussions should not be taken lightly. Neurosurgeons and other brain-injury experts emphasize that although some concussions are less serious than others, there is no such thing as a 'minor concussion.' 99

—American Association of Neurological Surgeons, "Concussion," December 2011. www.aans.org.

The American Association of Neurological Surgeons is dedicated to advancing the specialty of neurological surgery in order to promote the highest quality of patient care.

Facts and Illustrations

What Are the Risks of Concussions?

- The American Association of Neurological Surgeons states that concussions and other traumatic brain injuries cause more than **fifty thousand** deaths each year.

- According to the National Dissemination Center for Children with Disabilities, each year for children from birth to age fourteen, traumatic brain injuries result in **435,000** trips to the emergency room, **37,000** hospitalizations, and nearly **2,700** deaths.

- A study published in September 2012 found that professional **football players** had a risk of developing Alzheimer's disease and a degenerative neurological condition known as **ALS** at four times the rate of the general population—a risk believed to be linked to **repeated football-related head injuries**.

- According to the CDC, concussions and other traumatic brain injuries can increase the risk for conditions that become more prevalent with age, such as **Alzheimer's disease** and **Parkinson's disease**.

- A 2012 study published in the *American Journal of Sports Medicine* showed that younger athletes and those who were **female** showed more symptoms and took longer to recover from a concussion than older or male athletes.

- According to the Mayo Clinic, people who have sustained a concussion double their risk of developing **epilepsy** within the first five years after the injury.

Concussed Athletes Often Return to Play Too Quickly

A survey published in April 2012 by researchers from Columbus, Ohio, found that most high school athletes who have sustained concussions returned to play within three weeks—but a disturbing number returned too soon. This can be dangerous, as athletes whose brains are not fully healed after a concussion risk developing a deadly condition known as second-impact syndrome. This graph shows the length of time until return to play for high school athletes by sport.

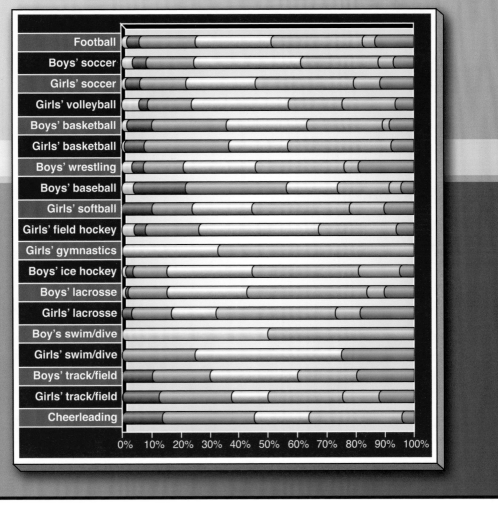

Legend: ■ <1 day □ 1–2 days ■ 3–6 days □ 7–9 days ■ 10–21 days □ >22 days ■ Other

Source: Mallika Marar et al. "Epidemiology of Concussions Among United States High School Athletes in 20 Sports," *American Journal of Sports Medicine*, April 2012. www.udel.edu.

CTE Destroys the Brain

One of the most devastating risks associated with multiple concussions or repeated blows to the head is chronic traumatic encephalopathy, or CTE. The disease, which has been closely linked to participation in boxing, football, and hockey, results in a steady, progressive decline of brain function. This illustration shows the symptoms of early-stage and advanced CTE.

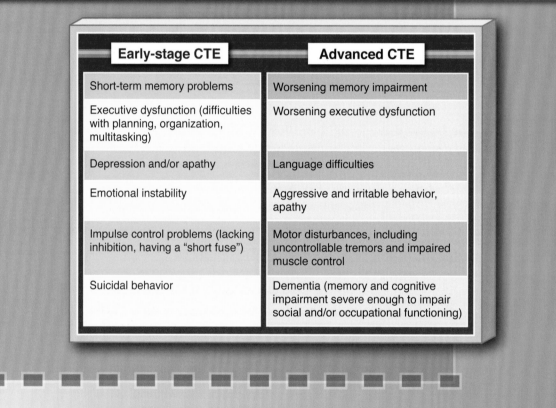

Early-stage CTE	Advanced CTE
Short-term memory problems	Worsening memory impairment
Executive dysfunction (difficulties with planning, organization, multitasking)	Worsening executive dysfunction
Depression and/or apathy	Language difficulties
Emotional instability	Aggressive and irritable behavior, apathy
Impulse control problems (lacking inhibition, having a "short fuse")	Motor disturbances, including uncontrollable tremors and impaired muscle control
Suicidal behavior	Dementia (memory and cognitive impairment severe enough to impair social and/or occupational functioning)

Source: Robert A. Stern et al. "Long-Term Consequences of Repetitive Brain Trauma: Chronic Traumatic Encephalopathy," *PM&R*, October 2011. www.bu.edu.

- The National Athletic Trainers Association states that **50 percent** of second-impact syndrome cases **result in death**.

- According to neurosurgeon and concussion expert Richard G. El-lenbogen, concussions can have a poor effect on a student's **academic performance**.

- According to the Brain Injury Research Institute, high school athletes have a **three-fold** higher risk of getting a second concussion once they have had a concussion.

- The American Association of Neurological Surgeons states that every year **eighty thousand to ninety thousand** people experience the onset of long-term or lifelong disabilities associated with concussions and other traumatic brain injuries.

- A US military study published in 2012 found that soldiers who sustained concussions while serving in Iraq or Afghanistan suffered from chronic, severe headaches at a rate **four to five times higher** than the general population.

- According to the Sports Concussion Institute, concussions in youth can be more damaging than those in adults because the **frontal lobe** area of the brain does not fully develop until age twenty-five.

- According to the American Association of Neurological Surgeons, people aged **sixty and older have the highest death rate** from concussion and other traumatic injuries, primarily because of falls, which become more prevalent as people age.

- In 2013 the National Institutes of Health (NIH) announced the results of a study on the brain of Junior Seau, a star NFL linebacker who died of a self-inflicted gunshot wound in 2012. The NIH study revealed **abnormalities consistent with chronic traumatic encephalopathy** (CTE). According to the NIH, similar findings have been "recently reported in autopsies of individuals with exposure to repetitive head injury, including professional and amateur athletes who played contact sports, individuals with multiple concussions, and veterans exposed to blast injury and other trauma."

Can Sports-Related Concussions Be Prevented?

> **The great challenge for the next generation of sports medicine experts will be to develop systematic methods to prevent concussion in sports.**
>
> —Lyle J. Micheli, director of the Division of Sports Medicine at Boston Children's Hospital.

> **What we really need to prevent concussions are seatbelts and airbags for our brains inside of our skulls.**
>
> —Andrew M. Blecher, a sports medicine physician at the Southern California Orthopedic Institute.

For years the NFL was the target of scathing criticism for its lackadaisical attitude about player concussions. The organization continually refused to acknowledge any relationship between football and long-term brain damage, arguing that there was no definitive proof showing a connection. That blatantly flawed perspective was proved wrong in 2009. A study commissioned by the NFL showed that Alzheimer's disease and/or other degenerative brain disorders were being diagnosed in former pro football players at a rate that was nineteen times higher than that of males in the general population. After the findings were announced, neurosurgeon Julian Bailes, who codirects the Brain Injury Research Institute, stated: "This is a game-changer—the whole debate, the ball's now in the N.F.L.'s court. They always say, 'We're going to do our own studies.' And now they have."[55]

Changing Football

Following the study, NFL commissioner Roger Goodell began pushing for changes in league rules that would help reduce the incidence of concussions. One major change was imposing stiff fines against players who make dangerous hits, especially deliberate helmet-to-helmet contact. Another change was the declaration that play stop immediately if a runner's helmet comes off during a play. Then came a new kickoff rule, which was implemented at the beginning of the 2011 football season. Kickoffs would take place at the 35-yard line rather than the 30-yard line. This was intended to eliminate most kick returns, which present a high risk of injury due to their violent and chaotic nature. According to NFL officials, these and other changes had the desired effect: concussions among NFL players dropped 12.5 percent in a year, from 218 in 2010 to 190 in 2011.

In September 2012 Goodell announced that the NFL had donated $30 million to the National Institutes of Health (NIH). At the NIH's discretion, the money will be allocated for research on concussions and other serious medical conditions. In an interview following the announcement, Goodell said that progress had been made but it was still not enough: "Well, there's a lot more work to be done, is the bottom line. There's a much greater awareness about head injuries and concussions and the importance of treating them conservatively and cautiously. . . . What we want to continue to do is be a part of that solution. And we expect that this is a shared responsibility that we all have to do more."[56]

A Model School

Mater Dei High School, a private school in Santa Ana, California, is often referred to as a football powerhouse. With fourteen league championships and five state titles since 1991, Mater Dei's football program is consistently ranked among the best in the country—and the school is also a national leader in concussion prevention. Safety is a top priority for the coaching staff, and they are fiercely committed to keeping their players safe. One of their main strategies is to make prevention a team effort. An ongoing challenge is honest reporting; the players are reluctant to speak up if they are hurt, because they want to stay in the game. As a result, coaches insist that the kids monitor each other and tell one of the staff if they suspect a teammate has been concussed. Says Mike Fernandez, Mater Dei's athletic trainer: "I'm not going to be able to see every hit. It's a crowded field with lots of contact. That's why we make it clear that monitoring concussions is the responsibility of the entire team. If a buddy is out of it and you don't tell us, that's on you."[57]

> " A study commissioned by the NFL showed that Alzheimer's disease and/or other degenerative brain disorders were being diagnosed in former pro football players at a rate that was nineteen times higher than that of males in the general population. "

In addition to the team-responsibility philosophy about concussions, the Mater Dei athletic department has enacted other measures as part of its concussion program. Baseline testing is in place to evaluate whether players have sustained a concussion and also to ensure that concussed players do not return to the game before they are completely healed. Football practice has been changed, with an approach that is much less physical and with fewer tackles. This cuts down significantly on the number of hits, which can help prevent head injuries. Overall, there is a general awareness that everyone at Mater Dei plays a role in keeping the players healthy and safe. "I look back and I can't believe the way it used to be," says Fernandez. "I think there used to be an attitude that concussions were an inevitable part of football, like ankle sprains. And maybe they are. But we still need to do everything possible to keep them from happening."[58]

Prevention or Hype?

One of the ways the Mater Dei athletic department helps protect football players is with top-of-the-line equipment. Their helmets are Riddell Revolution Speed, which feature inflatable pads inside that are designed to reduce the risk of concussion. These helmets were part of a three-year study of more than two thousand high school football players conducted by the University of Pittsburgh Medical Center (UPMC). The study, which was published in February 2006, found that athletes who wore

Riddell Revolution Speed helmets were 31 percent less likely to suffer a concussion than those who wore other types of helmets. In a news release announcing the findings, lead researcher Michael Collins, executive director of the UPMC Center for Sports Medicine, stated: "This study, the first to look at how the newer designed helmets performed in the field under real circumstances, provides preliminary evidence that the new helmet technology might substantially reduce, though certainly not prevent, the occurrence and incidence of concussion in high school football players."[59]

A more recent study, published in 2011, was conducted by researchers at Virginia Polytechnic Institute and State University (Virginia Tech). A decade ago, using sensors fitted to the insides of helmets, the team began compiling data from more than 1 million head impacts sustained by Virginia Tech players during football practices and games. From these statistics, the researchers could calculate the speeds and tackling angles that would most likely lead to concussions. They tested the safety features of ten different helmets, and the data yielded a STAR (Summation of Tests for the Analysis of Risk) value. From that data, the researchers created a rating system. The only helmet to receive five stars was the Riddell Revolution Speed, although several helmets by Schutt and Xenith also received high ratings for reducing concussion risk.

> **Mater Dei's football program is consistently ranked among the best in the country —and the school is also a national leader in concussion prevention.**

The claim that any helmet—no matter how high-tech it is—can reduce concussion risk is highly controversial. Many brain trauma experts say that even though protective equipment is essential to keep athletes safe, concussions occur inside the skull when the brain is propelled forward and backward, and no helmet can prevent the brain's motion. Jeffrey Kutcher, a neurologist who is chair of the American Academy of Neurology's Sports Neurology section, testified before a US Senate committee in October 2011 that all products being marketed for concussion prevention did not live up to that claim. Kutcher explained to committee members that although helmets had dramatically reduced the incidence of skull fracture, they could not prevent concussions. He stated:

> Every week I am asked by patients, parents, and coaches about the claims they hear and what equipment they should buy to prevent concussions. I wish there was such a product on the market. The simple truth is that no current helmet, mouthguard, headband, or other piece of equipment can significantly prevent concussions from occurring. They occur as the result of the nature of sports. Concussion prevention is much more about teaching proper technique, playing by the rules, and limiting the overall dose of impacts.[60]

Making Cheer Safer

According to a 2012 report by researchers at Ohio State University, cheerleading ranks seventeenth out of twenty sports for overall injuries. When ranking is based on the incidence of concussions, cheer moves up to twelfth place—and when including concussions that occur during practice, the only two sports that have higher rates are football and wrestling. A major reason for cheer's high concussion rate is a stunt called the double twist to a cradle, better known as the double down. A cheerleader is tossed into the air, performs two full twists, and lands in the arms of other cheerleaders. Performing this stunt during a January 2012 practice session led to a concussion for fifteen-year-old Madison DiGioia. She was the "flier" in a double down, and during her landing the back of her head smacked into the bent knee of one of the girls catching her. The pain was excruciating, she says: "like being stabbed in the back of the head."[61] It took two months before DiGioia's brain was fully healed, and she missed five weeks of school.

Because the concussion risk is so high, in April 2012 the national governing bodies of high school sports and cheerleading banned the double down for high school cheerleaders. Concussion specialist Robert Franks, who treated DiGioia, was not at all unhappy to hear about the rule change. He says he has seen "a large, increasing number" of cheerleaders with concussions, as he explains: "They're the population we're really keeping a close eye on because of increasing numbers. Programs are becoming more aggressive and routines are more complicated and cause injuries and mistakes."[62]

Legislating Safety

In May 2009 Washington became the first state to pass legislation intended to prevent concussions among young athletes. The law requires that when an athlete has suffered an apparent head injury, either during a game or at practice, he or she cannot return to play without the approval of a licensed medical professional. While Governor Christine Gregoire signed the bill, sixteen-year-old Zackery Lystedt watched, as did fifty of his friends and family members. "Out of tragedy," Gregoire said, "comes something good."[63] With her mention of "tragedy," the governor was referring to a catastrophic event that happened when Lystedt was thirteen years old and changed his life forever.

In October 2006 Lystedt was a member of the Tahoma Junior High School football team in Maple Valley, Washington. During a game, while tackling an opposing player, he slammed the back of his head on the ground. Lystedt lay on the field, rocking back and forth in pain, clutching the sides of his helmet with both hands. Officials rushed over and helped him back to the bench, where he sat out the final three plays of the first half. Because the school employed no athletic trainer, decisions about player injuries were left up to the coaching staff. So when Lystedt, who was known for being a fierce competitor, said he wanted to keep playing, the coach let him back in the game after halftime.

> " Many brain trauma experts say that even though protective equipment is essential to keep athletes safe, concussions occur inside the skull when the brain is propelled forward and backward, and no helmet can stop that from happening. "

At the end of the game, Lystedt made a tackle that helped clinch his team's win, and he was swarmed by his teammates—but then disaster struck. He turned to his father and said, "Dad, my head hurts really bad," then he lost consciousness and collapsed. When he briefly came to, he said: "Dad, I can't see."[64] Lystedt was airlifted to a Seattle hospital, where doctors performed emergency surgery by removing part of his skull to relieve swelling in his brain. Although they were able to save his life, the teen suffered numerous strokes and came perilously close to dying. He spent a week on life support, three months in a coma, and a year at a specialized rehabilitation facility in Dallas, Texas. When he returned home he still required round-the-clock care and went through grueling physical therapy sessions.

> " In May 2009 Washington became the first state to pass legislation intended to prevent concussions among young athletes. "

Today Lystedt is aware that he defied the doctors' predictions by making the progress that he has, and he is passionate about preventing other athletes from suffering the the effects of concussions. Largely because of his efforts and those of his family, more than forty states and the District of Columbia have adopted youth concussion laws. His goal is for this sort of legislation to be adopted by the remaining states so that kids all over the country are protected. Says his father, Victor Lystedt: "His purpose I think now in life is to change other people's lives."[65]

Room for Improvement

Society's attitude about concussions has come a long way since the time when athletes were hit in the head, sat a few minutes on the bench, and then returned to play. It is now known that concussions are serious brain injuries, and everything possible must be done to prevent them from happening. And a great deal has been done, from major rule changes in the NFL to better helmets and legislation designed to protect youth athletes. Still, concussions occur at an alarming rate every year, and brain trauma experts insist that more needs to be done to prevent them.

Can Sports-Related Concussions Be Prevented?

> **66 You can cut your risk of concussion in half by switching from the VSR4 [helmet] to the Xenith X1 [helmet]. 99**

—Stefan Duma in, "Virginia Tech Announces Football Helmet Ratings for Reducing Concussion Risk," Virginia Tech news release, May 10, 2011. www.eng.vt.edu.

Duma is a biomedical engineering professor at Virginia Tech.

> **66 Products that claim that they prevent concussions are borderline fraudulent, as there is NO study available that any current product can prevent concussions. 99**

—Dustin Fink, "Echoing 'Concussion Prevention' Concerns," *The Concussion Blog*, August 2, 2012. http://theconcussionblog.com.

Fink is a certified athletic trainer from Illinois who has spent more than twelve years working with athletes who have suffered concussions.

Primary Source Quotes

"We cannot eliminate head trauma from youth sports. What we can change is our mind-set so protecting the head and the brain is always a top consideration."

—Robert C. Cantu, "Preventing Sports Concussions Among Children," *New York Times*, October 6, 2012. www.nytimes.com.

Cantu is a Boston neurosurgeon and world-renowned expert on sports-related concussions who cofounded the Sports Legacy Institute and the Center for the Study of Traumatic Encephalopathy at Boston University School of Medicine.

"Unfortunately, there is no scientific, medically proven way of preventing a concussion."

—William Paul Meehan III, *Kids, Sports, and Concussions*. Santa Barbara, CA: ABC-CLIO, 2011.

Meehan is director of the Sports Concussion Clinic in the Division of Sports Medicine at Boston Children's Hospital.

"Helmets do not prevent concussions or sub-concussions from damaging the brain. We have to take the head out of the game. We have to change the rules."

—Bennet Omalu, "Head and Other Injuries in Youth, High School, College and Professional Football," oral statement at the US Congress judiciary forum, February 1, 2010. www.braininjuryresearchinstitute.org.

Omalu is a neuropathologist and codirector of the Brain Injury Research Institute at West Virginia University.

"Attention to safety, making your home safe, wearing a seatbelt while in a car, and wearing a properly designed helmet during sports activities are crucial to preventing concussion."

—Ryszard M. Pluta, "Concussion," *Journal of the American Medical Association*, July 6, 2011. http://jama.jamanetwork.com.

Pluta is a physician with the National Institute of Neurological Disorders and Stroke.

"Public education is important in raising awareness for concussion and its complications."

—Benjamin Wedro, "Concussion," MedicineNet, August 27, 2012. www.medicinenet.com.

Wedro is an emergency medicine physician at Gundersen Clinic, a regional trauma center in La Crosse, Wisconsin.

"Undoubtedly, the most important safety and injury prevention issue in sports today is concussions and repetitive head trauma."

—Ken Reed, "Concussion Research Can't Be Ignored," *The Sport Digest* (blog), September 1, 2011. http://thesportdigest.com.

Reed is a physician and sports policy director for the sports reform organization League of Fans.

"There are strategies that can be used to prevent concussions. . . . Appropriate protective equipment can be used to protect the brain, and improvements to existing protective equipment could be made to improve current technologies."

—Vikas Kapil, "Protecting School-Age Athletes from Sports-Related Concussion Injury," CDC congressional testimony, September 8, 2010. www.cdc.gov.

Kapil is an emergency medicine and public health physician.

Can Sports-Related Concussions Be Prevented?

- A 2011 study by researchers from Maryland and Virginia found that concussion rates for **helmeted sports** (football, boys' lacrosse) were nearly twice that of non-helmeted sports such as basketball and soccer.

- Strategies that brain trauma expert Robert C. Cantu recommends to help prevent concussions among athletes under age fourteen is **no tackle football** before that age, **no body checking** in youth hockey, and **no heading** in soccer.

- According to the NFL, a rule change that moved the kickoff to the 35-yard-line from the 30-yard line during the 2011 season resulted in a **40 percent** decline in concussions during kickoff returns.

- In an effort to prevent concussions, the Pop Warner youth football organization **banned head-to-head hits** in 2011.

- According to a study published in November 2011 by researchers from the Cleveland Clinic, **modern plastic football helmets** are no more effective at preventing concussions than the leather helmets worn by athletes in the early 1900s.

- In 2011, to help prevent head injuries among players, the NHL introduced Rule 48, which levies stiff penalties for **deliberate hits to an opposing player's head**.

Young Athletes Protected by Law

As of October 2012, forty-one US states had adopted laws designed to prevent concussions among young athletes and to specify the protocol to be followed if an athlete is suspected of being concussed. Shown on this map are those states, as well as the states with pending legislation and those with no legislation.

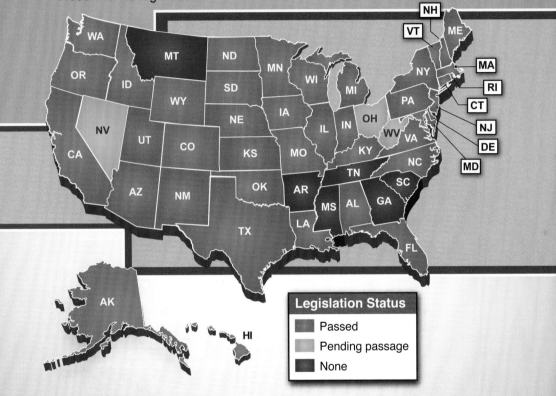

Source: NFL Evolution, "Concussion Legislation by State," October 2012. www.nflevolution.com.

- According to Toronto, Canada, neurosurgeon and concussion expert Charles H. Tator, **banning hits to the head** in all levels of hockey would help prevent concussions.

- Because of the high concussion risk, in 2011 the American Academy of Pediatrics issued an official statement that it **opposed boxing** as a sport for children and adolescents.

Pro Football Players on Concussion Safety

Since 2009 the National Football League has made a number of rule and procedural changes designed to reduce the risk of concussions. In December 2011 the Associated Press conducted a poll of NFL players to gauge whether concussion safety and attitudes about head injuries have changed, and this graph shows how they responded.

Question	Player Responses (44 participants)	
Specifically with regard to concussions, is playing in the NFL safer, more dangerous, or the same as it was in 2009 when the issue first began to get a lot of attention?	Safer	28
	Same	13
	More dangerous	2
	Not sure	1
If you get what you think could be a concussion, do you think you would hide it and try to stay in the game or immediately pull yourself out?	Hide it	23
	Immediately leave	21
Is that a change from 2009?	Yes	7
	No	26
	No answer	11
Can more be done to protect players from head injuries?	Yes	18
	No	24
	No answer	2
Should the NFL have independent neurologists at games to examine players and determine whether they should be held out because of concussions?	Yes	31
	No	10
	No answer	3

Source: Associated Press, "Results of Concussion Survey," ESPN, December 26, 2011. http://espn.go.com.

- According to the National Athletic Trainers Association, only **42 percent** of US high schools have access to athletic trainers/sports medicine specialists.

Parents Divided on Youth Football

To help prevent concussions among young athletes, brain trauma experts emphasize that kids should not play tackle football until they are at least fourteen years old. During an ESPN survey conducted during the summer or 2012, one thousand parents were asked their opinions about age requirements for their sons to play tackle football. Their answers varied widely depending on whether they were professional football fans.

In your opinion, what should the minimum age requirement be for kids to play full-contact football?

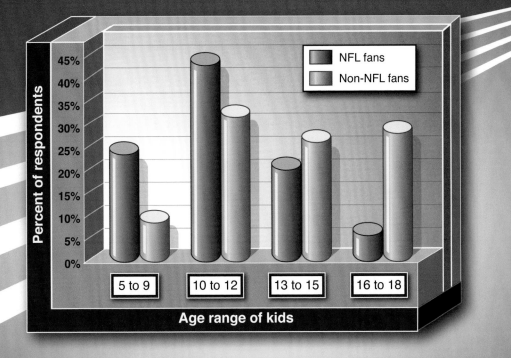

Source: Paula Lavigne, "Concussion News Worries Parents," ESPN, August 26, 2012. http://espn.go.com.

- As of October 2012, forty-one US states and Washington, DC, had **youth sport–safety laws** in place that were designed to help prevent concussions among young athletes.

Key People and Advocacy Groups

Sanford H. Auerbach: A prominent Boston University School of Medicine neurologist who in 1988 coined the term *post-concussive syndrome* to describe a condition in which concussion symptoms linger for weeks or months following a concussion.

Robert C. Cantu: A Boston neurosurgeon and noted expert on sports-related concussions who cofounded both the Sports Legacy Institute and the Center for the Study of Traumatic Encephalopathy at Boston University School of Medicine.

Ira Casson: A neurologist from New York and former cochair of the NFL's panel on head injuries who was strongly criticized for denying the connection between repeated blows to the heads of pro football players and degenerative brain disease.

Dignity After Football: An organization that is committed to representing the rights of retired and disabled former NFL players, many of whom suffer from long-term brain damage from football-related head injuries.

Roger Goodell: Commissioner of the NFL since 2006, Goodell was sharply criticized for the league's neglect in its management of active and retired players with brain injuries and was subsequently instrumental in getting tougher laws passed to guard against concussions.

Robert E. Harbaugh and Richard L. Saunders: Neurology specialists who coined the term *second-impact syndrome* in 1984 to describe the catastrophic brain injury that can result if someone who has had a concussion sustains a second blow to the head.

David Allen Hovda: The director of the Brain Injury Research Center at the University of California–Los Angeles, who is known for his profound discoveries about how concussions affect the brain.

Eric Lindros: A professional hockey star who retired in 2007 at age thirty-four and who has spoken publicly about the harmful effects that multiple concussions have had on his life.

Ann McKee: A professor of neurology and pathology at Boston University School of Medicine and codirector of the school's Center for the Study of Traumatic Encephalopathy.

National Collegiate Athletic Association (NCAA): Represents and oversees twenty-three collegiate sports, provides support to its members, enforces NCAA bylaws, and implements/monitors concussion management policies for athletes.

Bennet Omalu: A world-renowned neuropathologist and brain trauma expert who discovered abnormal deposits of the protein tau in the brain of deceased pro football player Mike Webster; his discovery marked the beginning of research into chronic traumatic encephalopathy.

Sports Legacy Institute: An organization that seeks to solve the concussion crisis in sports and the military through medical research, treatment, education, and prevention.

Tom Udall: A US senator from New Mexico who is a staunch advocate of improving standards for youth football helmets and other safety equipment and who calls for harsh penalties against manufacturers who make false claims about their products.

Chronology

1905

After the deaths of eighteen college football players in one season, US president Theodore Roosevelt summons sports leaders from Harvard, Princeton, and Yale to the White House for a summit on college football safety reform.

1973

In a paper titled "The Aftermath of Boxing," prominent British physician John Arthur Nicholas Corsellis describes the devastating brain damage he discovered during post-mortem examinations of the brains of fifteen former boxers.

2000

Neurologist Barry Jordan and neurosurgeon Julian Bailes publish a study of nearly eleven hundred former pro football players that found more than 60 percent suffered at least one concussion during their careers, and 26 percent had three or more concussions.

1900   **1930**   **1970**   **2000**

1984

In a paper titled "The Second Impact in Catastrophic Contact-Sports Head Trauma," neurosurgeon Richard L. Saunders and neurologist Robert E. Harbaugh coin the term *second-impact syndrome* to describe the catastrophic brain injury that can result if someone who has had a concussion sustains a second blow to the head.

1990

The Colorado Medical Society publishes a document titled "Guidelines for the Management of Concussion in Sports," which calls for immediate field evaluation of athletes who are suspected of suffering a concussion.

1928

New Jersey forensic pathologist Harrison S. Martland publishes a paper titled "Punch Drunk," in which he describes the long-term brain damage of prizefighters who are repeatedly punched in the head during boxing matches.

1988

Boston University School of Medicine neurologist Sanford H. Auerbach coins the term *post-concussive syndrome* to describe a condition in which symptoms linger for weeks or months following a concussion.

2001

The first International Symposium on Concussion in Sport is held in Vienna, Austria; experts who attend are charged with providing recommendations for improvement of the safety and health of athletes who suffer concussive injuries in ice hockey, football, soccer, and other sports.

2008

The Center for the Study of Traumatic Encephalopathy is founded at Boston University School of Medicine.

2010

The youth football organization Pop Warner establishes a rule that any athlete who has sustained a head injury must obtain a note from a licensed medical professional who is trained in concussion management before returning to play.

2005

A University of North Carolina study finds that nearly 18 percent of retired NFL players who had at least one concussion during their careers suffer from permanent thinking or memory impairment.

2005

2010

2002

During an autopsy on retired pro football player Mike Webster, neuropathologist Bennet Omalu discovers dark spots on Webster's brain that prove to be abnormal deposits of a protein associated with dementia. This marks the beginning of research into the degenerative brain condition known as chronic traumatic encephalopathy (CTE).

2011

The NFL donates $30 million to the NIH for medical research focused on brain injuries and to help establish the Sports and Health Research Program.

2009

Washington becomes the first state to pass legislation mandating that athletes under age eighteen who have suffered a concussion cannot return to play without written permission from a certified medical professional. That same year, the NFL imposes its own rules about when players should be allowed to return to games or practices after head injuries.

2012

A study by researchers from Michigan State University reveals that female athletes and younger athletes take longer to recover from concussions than male athletes and older athletes. Based on this finding, the team urges physicians and athletic trainers to take gender and age into consideration when dealing with concussion injuries.

Related Organizations

Brain Injury Association of America (BIAA)

1608 Spring Hill Rd., Suite 110
Vienna, VA 22182
phone: (703) 761-0750 • fax: (703) 761-0755
e-mail: info@biausa.org • website: www.biausa.org

The BIAA is the oldest and largest brain injury advocacy organization in the United States. Its website offers news releases, *The Challenge!* quarterly newsletter, a section with detailed information about brain injuries, and a fact sheet about sports-related concussions.

Brain Trauma Foundation

7 World Trade Center, 34th Floor
250 Greenwich St.
New York, NY 10007
phone: (212) 772-0608
e-mail: info@braintrauma.org • website: www.braintrauma.org

The Brain Trauma Foundation is dedicated to scientific research and to educating the public about concussions. Its website features news articles, a glossary, research updates, and a number of other concussion-related publications.

Center for Brain Health

2200 W. Mockingbird Ln.
Dallas, TX 75235
phone: (214) 905-3007 • fax: (214) 905-3026
website: www.brainhealth.utdallas.edu

Through breakthrough research and treatment, the mission of the Center for Brain Health is to understand, protect, and heal the brain. Its website offers research papers, testimonials, archived news releases, a link to the organization's blog, and a search engine that produces numerous results for material about concussions.

Related Organizations

Center for the Study of Traumatic Encephalopathy (CSTE)

Boston University School of Medicine
72 E. Concord St.
Robinson Complex, Suite 7380
Boston, MA 02118
phone: (617) 638-8491
e-mail: cste@bu.edu • website: www.bu.edu/cste

The CSTE is a research center that is devoted to increasing awareness and understanding of the degenerative brain disease CTE. Its website features case studies, research papers, news releases, and many articles about concussion that are accessible through the search engine.

Centers for Disease Control and Prevention (CDC)

1600 Clifton Rd.
Atlanta, GA 30333
phone: (800) 232-4636
e-mail: cdcinfo@cdc.gov • website: www.cdc.gov

The CDC is dedicated to protecting health and promoting quality of life through the prevention and control of disease, injury, and disability. A wealth of information about concussions is available on its website, including research, statistics, and a variety of publications.

Defense and Veterans Brain Injury Center

National Headquarters
1335 East-West Hwy., Suite 6-100
Silver Spring, MD 20910
phone: (800) 870-9244
e-mail: info@dvbic.org • website: www.dvbic.org

The Defense and Veterans Brain Injury Center is the arm of the US military health system that is devoted to traumatic brain injuries. Its website offers concussion statistics, news articles, an "Educational Materials" section, and research publications.

National Athletic Trainers' Association (NATA)

2952 Stemmons Fwy. #200
Dallas, TX 75247
phone: (214) 637-6282 • fax: (214) 637-2206
e-mail: info@nata.org • website: www.nata.org

The NATA is a professional membership association for certified athletic trainers and others who support the athletic training profession. Numerous articles and resource materials are available through the website's search engine.

Sports Concussion Institute

5230 Pacific Concourse Dr., Suite 300
Los Angeles, CA 90045
phone: (310) 643-9595 • fax: (310) 643-5180
e-mail: info@concussiontreatment.com
website: www.concussiontreatment.com

The Sports Concussion Institute seeks to reduce the long-term impacts of concussions on athletes and to promote awareness and education of concussion prevention and management. The "Resources" section of its website offers extensive information about concussions for athletes, parents, teachers, coaches, and health-care professionals.

Sports Legacy Institute

PO Box 181225
Boston, MA 02118
phone: (781) 819-5706 • fax: (781) 819-5710
e-mail: info@sportslegacy.org • website: http://sportslegacy.org

The Sports Legacy Institute is committed to solving the concussion crisis in sports and the military through medical research, treatment, education, and prevention. A wide array of articles and publications about concussions is available on its website for athletes, parents, coaches, health-care professionals, and the community.

For Further Research

Books

Linda Bickerstaff, *Frequently Asked Questions About Concussions*. New York: Rosen, 2010.

Colleen Butler, *Concussion Recovery: Rebuilding the Injured Brain*. Victoria, British Columbia: Hidden Lighthouse, 2012.

Robert C. Cantu and Mark Hyman, *Concussions and Our Kids*. New York: Houghton Mifflin Harcourt, 2012.

Linda Carroll and David Rosner, *The Concussion Crisis: Anatomy of a Silent Epidemic*. New York: Simon & Schuster, 2011.

Mary Lee Kamberg, *Sports Concussions*. New York: Rosen, 2011.

William Paul Meehan III, *Kids, Sports, and Concussions*. Santa Barbara, CA: ABC-CLIO, 2011.

Periodicals

Katie Abbondanza, "Heady Business," *Girls' Life*, August/September 2012.

Lenny Bernstein, "Why We Should Step Up Vigilance of Concussions in Teen Girls," *Washington Post*, April 5, 2011.

Bob Bolles, "One Hit Too Many," *Circle Track*, October 2012.

Robert C. Cantu, "Preventing Sports Concussions Among Children," *New York Times*, October 6, 2012.

Sean Conboy, "Sidney Crosby and the Human Car Wreck," *Pittsburgh Magazine*, March 2011.

Guy Falotico, "Headlong off Trouble: Concussions Can Be More than Just a Headache," *Current Health Teens*, a *Weekly Reader* publication, November 2010.

Kate Huvane Gamble, "A New Game Plan for Concussion," *Neurology Now*, February/March 2011.

Lauren Gelman, "A Head Injury You Should Never Ignore," *Prevention*, January 2011.

Dan Keane, "The Warm Roar and Bottomless Sadness of Brain Injury," *Atlantic*, May 2012.

Austin Murphy, "Hard Times in the Endangered Zone," *Sports Illustrated*, November 7, 2011.

Ryan Pyette, "Concussions Take Toll on Teen Hockey Player," *Edmonton (Alberta) Sun*, September 9, 2011.

Lauren Tarshis, "Head Trauma," *Scholastic Scope*, October 10, 2011.

Matt Terl, "Concussion in Youth Sports: Dealing with a Dangerous Headache," *Parks & Recreation*, December 2011.

Lindsay Tice, "Cheerleader's Injury Reveals Complexity, Dangers of Concussions," *Bangor (ME) Daily News*, April 3, 2011.

Kirsten Weir, "Hard Hit: Is Football Too Violent for the Health of Its Players?," *Current Science*, a *Weekly Reader* publication, October 14, 2011.

Internet Sources

Andrew M. Blecher, "Is 'Preventing Concussions' False Advertising?," *NFL Concussion Litigation* (blog), May 21, 2012. http://nflconcussionlitigation.com/?p=701.

Cory Hatch, "Docs Cite Head Injuries in Ruling Out Youth Boxing," *My Health News Daily*, August 29, 2011. www.myhealthnewsdaily.com/1625-boxing-dangerous-for-kids.html.

Chris Jones, "How Concussions Work," HowStuffWorks, 2012. http://science.howstuffworks.com/environmental/life/inside-the-mind/human-brain/concussion.htm.

Ray Legendre and Jacques Von Lunen, "Concussions Can Be Life-Altering for Student Athletes," *Vancouver, WA Columbian,* "Live Well," September 1, 2012. www.columbian.com/news/2012/sep/01/concussions-student-athletes-impact.

Ranit Mishori, "Youth Sports Injuries: What a Headache!," *Huffington Post*, "Healthy Living," August 29, 2012. www.huffingtonpost.com/ranit-mishori-md-mhs/concussions-sports_b_1837251.html.

Rachel Rettner, "Teenage Brains Particularly Vulnerable to Concussions," *My Health News Daily*, February 28, 2012. www.myhealthnewsdaily.com/2288-teens-concussion-sports-head-injury.html.

Source Notes

Overview

1. Quoted in Ray Legendre and Jacques Von Lunen, "Concussions Can Be Life-Altering for Student Athletes," *Vancouver, WA Columbian*, "Live Well," September 1, 2012. www.columbian.com.
2. Keith Black, *Brain Surgeon*. New York: Wellness Central-Hatchett Book Group, 2009, p. xi.
3. Andrew M. Blecher, "Guest Post: Is 'Preventing Concussions' False Advertising?," NFL Concussion Litigation, May 21, 2012. http://nflconcussionlitigation.com.
4. Rosemarie Scolaro Moser, *Ahead of the Game*. Lebanon, NH: University Press of New England, 2012, p. 29.
5. Quoted in *Neurology Now*, "A New Game Plan," February/March 2011, p. 30.
6. Mehmet Oz, "Playing Defense," *Time*, February 3, 2011. www.time.com.
7. Jeffrey Kluger, "Headbanger Nation," *Time*, February 3, 2011. www.time.com.
8. Ken Reed, "Concussion Research Can't Be Ignored," *The Sport Digest* (blog), September 1, 2011. http://thesportdigest.com.
9. Quoted in Kate Snow et al. "Concussion Crisis Growing in Girls' Soccer," NBC News, *Rock Center*, May 9, 2012. http://rockcenter.nbcnews.com.
10. Quoted in Laura Beil, "A Smack Upside the Head," *Men's Health*, January 25, 2012. www.menshealth.com.
11. William Paul Meehan III, *Kids, Sports, and Concussions*. Santa Barbara, CA: ABC-CLIO, 2011, p. 30.
12. Quoted in Snow et al. "Concussion Crisis Growing in Girls' Soccer."
13. Quoted in Anahad O'Connor, "Concussions May Be More Severe in Girls and Young Athletes," *Well* (blog), *New York Times*, May 10, 2012. http://well.blogs.nytimes.com.
14. William Paul Meehan III, "Studying the Effects of Multiple Concussions," *Thriving* (blog), March 19, 2012. http://childrenshospitalblog.org.
15. Robert C. Cantu, interviewed by Michelle Healy, "Parents' Vigilance Can Head Off Kids' Concussion Risk," *USA Today*, September 29, 2012. www.usatoday.com.
16. Mandy Huggins, "NFL Concussion Litigation: A Doctor's Perspective," *Ruling Sports* (blog), July 30, 2012. http://rulingsports.com.
17. Lacey, "My Concussion Still Sucks Metaphorical Balls," *My Life of Cards* (blog), June 15, 2012. http://mylifeofcards.wordpress.com.
18. American Association of Neurological Surgeons, "Concussion," December 2011. www.aans.org.
19. Meehan, *Kids, Sports, and Concussions*, p. 55.
20. Quoted in Reed, "Concussion Research Can't Be Ignored."
21. Reed, "Concussion Research Can't Be Ignored."

What Are Concussions?

22. Meehan, *Kids, Sports, and Concussions*, p. xviii.
23. Meehan, *Kids, Sports, and Concussions*, p. xvii.
24. Linda Carroll and David Rosner, *The Concussion Crisis: Anatomy of a Silent Epidemic*. New York: Simon & Schuster, 2011, p. 10.

25. Brain Injury Association of America, "Mild Brain Injury and Concussion." www.biausa .org.
26. Natalie Mackow, "Concussions in Athletes: To Play or Not to Play," Serendip Studio, April 2010. http://serendip.brynmawr.edu.
27. Robert C. Cantu, "Preventing Sports Concussions Among Children," *New York Times*, October 6, 2012. www.nytimes.com.
28. Moser, *Ahead of the Game*, p. 10.
29. Cantu, interviewed by Healy, "Parents' Vigilance Can Head Off Kids' Concussion Risk."
30. Sarah Parsons, "Challenges," *Under the Same Moon* (blog), June 29, 2012. http://forever underthesamemoon.blogspot.com.
31. Sarah Parsons, e-mail interview with author, October 7, 2012.
32. Quoted in Joaquin Sapien and Daniel Zwerdling, "Army Study Finds Troops Suffer Concussions in Training," ProPublica, August 24, 2012. www.propublica.org.

How Are Concussions Diagnosed and Treated?

33. Quoted in Mike Davis, "Lawrence Woman Speaks Out About the Dangers of Concussions," *Times of Trenton* (New Jersey), August 26, 2012. www.nj.com/times.
34. Quoted in Davis, "Lawrence Woman Speaks Out About the Dangers of Concussions."
35. Quoted in Steve Reed, "NASCAR News: Jeff Gordon Says He Would Have Kept Concussion Quiet, Unlike Dale Earnhardt Jr.," *Huffington Post*, October 13, 2012. www .huffingtonpost.com.
36. William Oates, *An Injury Prevention Curriculum for Coaches*. Stop Sports Injuries, Fall 2011. www.stopsportsinjuries.org.
37. Quoted in David Newton, "NASCAR Considers Neurological Tests," ESPN, October 16, 2012. http://espn.go.com.
38. Quoted in Newton, "NASCAR Considers Neurological Tests."
39. Gerald Tramontano, "Head Games," *New York Times*, September 12, 2008. www.ny times.com.
40. Tramontano, "Head Games."
41. Quoted in Lindsay Barton, "Proven Benefit Cognitive Plus Physical Rest," Sports CAPP, June 22, 2012. www.sportscapp.com.
42. Quoted in Kevin Simpson, "Treating Kids for Concussions Also Looks at Holistic Emotional Aspects," *Denver Post*, May 31, 2012. www.denverpost.com.
43. Quoted in Simpson, "Treating Kids for Concussions Also Looks at Holistic Emotional Aspects."

What Are the Risks of Concussions?

44. Dan Keane, interview with author, September 30, 2012.
45. Dan Keane, "The Warm Roar and Bottomless Sadness of Brain Injury," *Atlantic*, May 2012. www.theatlantic.com.
46. Keane, interview.
47. Quoted in Bob Bolles, "One Hit Too Many," *Circle Track*, August 2012. www.circle track.com.
48. Quoted in Bolles, "One Hit Too Many."
49. Quoted in Bolles, "One Hit Too Many."
50. Terry Zeigler, "Second Impact Syndrome," SportsMD, January 2, 2012. www.sportsmd .com.

51. Carroll and Rosner, *The Concussion Crisis*, p. 12.

52. Kluger "Headbanger Nation."

53. Quoted in Jeanne Marie Laskas, "Game Brain," *GQ*, October 2009. www.gq.com.

54. Laskas, "Game Brain."

Can Sports-Related Concussions Be Prevented?

55. Quoted in Alan Schwarz, "Dementia Risk Seen in Players in N.F.L. Study," *New York Times*, September 29, 2009. www.nytimes.com.

56. Roger Goodell, interviewed by Albert Breer, "Roger Goodell on Player Safety: We All Have to Do More," NFL.com, September 5, 2012. www.nfl.com.

57. Quoted in Jonah Lehrer, "The Fragile Teenage Brain," Grantland, January 10, 2010. www.grantland.com.

58. Quoted in Lehrer, "The Fragile Teenage Brain."

59. Quoted in University of Pittsburgh, Medical Center, news release. "Newer Football Helmet Design May Reduce Incidence of Concussions in High School Players, Shows University of Pittsburgh Study," January 9, 2006. www.upmc.com.

60. Jeffrey Kutcher, testimony before the US Senate Committee on Commerce, Science, and Transportation, October 19, 2011. www.aan.com.

61. Quoted in Michael Vitez, "Putting Heads First, Banning Cheerleading's Double-Down," *Philadelphia Inquirer*, April 1, 2012. http://articles.philly.com.

62. Quoted in Vitez, "Putting Heads First, Banning Cheerleading's Double-Down."

63. Quoted in Tom Wyrwich, "Gregoire: 'Out of Tragedy Comes Something Good,'" *Seattle Times*, May 15, 2009. http://seattletimes.com.

64. Quoted in Carroll and Rosner, *The Concussion Crisis*, p. 32.

65. Quoted in Sandra Hughes, "Teen Inspires 'Shake It Off' Law," CBS News, May 14, 2009. www.cbsnews.com.

List of Illustrations

Index

Note: boldface page numbers indicate illustrations

About the Author

Peggy J. Parks holds a bachelor of science degree from Aquinas College in Grand Rapids, Michigan, where she graduated magna cum laude. An author who has written more than one hundred educational books for children and young adults, Parks lives in Muskegon, Michigan, a town that she says inspires her writing because of its location on the shores of Lake Michigan.